The EU as a Global Player

A new look at the European Union's role as a global actor, with special focus on the theme of interregionalism in its relations with key regions around the world: Africa, Asia, South America, North America and Central-Eastern Europe.

This new collection clearly shows how, since the end of the Cold War, the European Union has gradually expanded its external relations and foreign policies and become a global actor in world politics. During the last decade interregionalism has become a key component of the EU's external relations and foreign policies. In fact, the EU has quickly become the hub of a large number of interregional arrangements with a number of regions around the world. Promoting regional and interregional relations not only justifies and enhances the EU's own existence and efficiency as a global 'player', the strategy also promotes the legitimacy and status of other regions, giving rise to a deepening of cross-cutting interregional relations in trade and economic relations, political dialogue, development cooperation, cultural relations and security cooperation.

This book was previously published as a special issue of the leading *Journal of European Integration*.

Fredrik Söderbaum is Associate Professor at the Department of Peace and Development Research, Göteborg University (Padrigu) and an Associate Research Fellow at the United Nations University/Comparative Regional Integration Studies (UNU/CRIS).

Luk van Langenhove is Professor and Director of the United Nations University/Comparative Regional Integration Studies (UNU/CRIS).

The EU as a Global Player

The Politics of Interregionalism

Edited by
Fredrik Söderbaum and Luk van Langenhove

Routledge
Taylor & Francis Group

LONDON AND NEW YORK

First published 2006 by Routledge
2 Park Square, Milton Park, Abingdon, Oxon, OX14 4RN

Simultaneously published in the USA and Canada
by Routledge
270 Madison Ave, New York, NY 10016

Routledge is an imprint of the Taylor & Francis Group, an informa business

Transferred to Digital Printing 2008

© 2006 Taylor & Francis Ltd

Typeset in Sabon by Genesis Typesetting Ltd, Rochester, Kent

British Library Cataloguing in Publication Data
A catalogue record for this book is available from the British Library

Library of Congress Cataloging in Publication Data
A catalog record for this book has been requested

ISBN10: 0-415-39735-9 (hbk)
ISBN10: 0-415-46390-4 (pbk)

ISBN13: 978-0-415-39735-6 (hbk)
ISBN13: 978-0-415-46390-4 (pbk)

CONTENTS

Preface

This book has its origins in a two-year research project funded by the Swedish Institute for European Policy Studies (SIEPS) on the overall theme of "The role of the EU in the world". As part of this project we invited some leading scholars to contribute to a special issue of the *Journal of European Integration* (JEI), vol. 27, no. 3 (2005) entitled "The EU as a Global Actor: The Role of Interregionalism".

Our group of authors has had many and at times intense meetings and conversations throughout the project. The majority of the contributors met to exchange views and discuss papers in a section on "States, Regions and Regional World Orders" at the 5th Pan-European International Relations Conference of the Standing Group of International Relations (SGIR) held in The Hague, 9–11 September 2004. The discussants and participants to that section are all gratefully acknowledged. We have, in particular, greatly benefited from the comments of Björn Hettne, who has reviewed all the papers, as well as from the inputs of all the anonymous reviewers.

We are also deeply indebted to Emil Kirchner, JEI's Executive Editor, for supporting the project from the beginning and later promoting the book at Routledge. And we extend our gratitude to JEI's editing team, Hans Michelmann and Susan Sydenham, for invaluable assistance, comments and not the least corrections. Warm thanks also to Ana-Christina Costea at UNU-CRIS for her assistance in helping out with the manuscript. Gratitude also goes to Amber Bulkley and the Routledge team for encouragement and support in the completion of the volume.

Fredrik Söderbaum and Luk van Langenhove, January 2006

Introduction: The EU as a Global Actor and the Role of Interregionalism

FREDRIK SÖDERBAUM* & LUK VAN LANGENHOVE**

1. The Theme

The European Union's external relations and foreign policies have expanded dramatically since the end of the Cold War and the establishment of the EU through the signing of the Treaty of Maastricht in 1993. Today the EU has relations with virtually every country and most regions in the world. The EU has become a force in international affairs, especially in trade, development cooperation, the promotion of regional integration, democracy and good governance, human rights and, to an increasing extent, also in security policies.

There are, however, many different views on what type of political animal the EU actually is and on the nature and impact of its external relations. Some critics argue that the EU has diffuse and ineffective foreign policies, based on no genuinely common values; in essence, that the EU is an incomplete or merely potential 'actor' on the world scene. Even among the proponents there are different interpretations about the nature of the EU's foreign policy and 'actorness'. As a result, the EU is perceived as an ambiguous polity (actor) and its foreign policy profile appears to be a moving target.

This collection aims to provide an insight into the EU's role in the world and as a global actor. It takes as its point of departure the fact that during the last decade there has been an increasing emphasis within the EU on interregionalism (region–to–region relations) as a foundation for its external policies. This foreign policy 'doctrine' is deeply rooted in the European Commission and has been expressed many times by a number of leading politicians and policy–makers during the last decade, albeit not always in the same way. As early as 1990 the then German Minister of Foreign Affairs, Hans–Dietrich Genscher, stated, with reference to interregionalism, that "the path of the political dialogue and economic cooperation embarked upon by the EC in a spirit of true partnership is proving to be the path of the future" (Edwards & Regelsberger 1990, vii–viii). More recently, in September 2001 an interregional model was proposed by the Belgian Prime Minister, Guy Verhofstadt, then President of the European Council, who suggested that the current G8 should be replaced by a G8 based on more adequate regional representation: "... we need to create a forum where the leading continental partnerships can all speak on an equal footing: the European Union, the African Union, the Common Market of the South (Mercosur), the Association of Southeast Asian Nations (ASEAN), the North American Free Trade Agreement (NAFTA), etc."[1]

Promoting and developing regional integration is a key feature of the relations between the EU and other regions in many parts of the world. The most developed relationship in Latin America is with Mercosur. The EU–Mercosur Interregional Framework Cooperation Agreement is seen as a step towards an Interregional Association Agreement and a strengthened interregional partnership between the EU and Mercosur (European Commission 1996).

In Asia, the EU is engaged in strong interregional relations with the Association of South East Asian Nations (ASEAN), and also offers support for the South Asian Association for Regional Cooperation (SAARC) focused on trade integration among South Asian countries. The EU's exchanges with ASEAN gave birth to a new institutional framework of interregional multidimensional relations with the creation of the Asia–Europe Meeting (ASEM) in 1996. The historical ASEM 5 Summit held in Hanoi in October

2004 marked the enlargement of ASEM from 26 to 39 partners through the accession of the ten new EU member states and three new countries from ASEAN that were not yet part of the process: Cambodia, Laos and Burma/Myanmar.

The EU has clearly acknowledged the link between regional integration and development in its policy towards the African, Caribbean and Pacific (ACP) countries by including regional integration among the three focal priorities for poverty reduction mentioned in the Cotonou Agreement. As stated in article 28 of the Agreement: "Cooperation shall provide effective assistance to achieve the objectives and priorities which the ACP States have set themselves in the context of regional and sub–regional cooperation and integration, including interregional and intra–ACP cooperation".[2] Given that the ACP framework comprises countries widely dispersed geographically, the EU has also developed more specific interregional partnerships with Central Africa, Eastern Africa, Southern Africa, the Caribbean and the Indian Ocean under the auspices of the Cotonou Agreement.

Thus, the EU is becoming the hub of a large number of interregional arrangements which, in turn, are strengthening its own regionalist ideology. Promoting regional and interregional relations not only justifies and enhances the EU's own existence and efficiency as an 'actor'; the strategy also promotes the legitimacy and status of other regions. This, in turn, promotes further crosscutting regionalism and interregionalism around the world. Most of these EU–promoted interregional arrangements encompass not only trade and economic relations but also political dialogue, development cooperation, cultural relations and security cooperation. The ambition of the EU is also to formalise as well as institutionalise the relations between two regional bodies (now often referred to as 'partnerships') but, for pragmatic reasons, the agreements with different counterpart regions show a "bewildering variety" (Hettne 2005).

The study of interregionalism is underrepresented in the academic debate and we simply do not know enough when and why interregionalism occurs and what it is actually an instance of. There is a pressing need to learn more about the 'why' and the 'hows' of interregionalism in the EU's foreign policy. This collection of studies is an attempt to provide more systematic and comparative research on this topic.

2. Purpose of the Studies

The overall aim of this collection of studies is to assess the EU as a global actor, with particular attention given to the role of interregionalism in its foreign policies towards some of the most important regions around the world: Africa, Asia, South America, North America and Eastern and Central Europe.

One of the central ambitions is to assess whether there is an increasing tendency of regions to assume a stronger role on the world scene and gain in 'actorness'. Our concern is first and foremost with the EU, but the degree of actorness of counterpart regions is also relevant. What brings actorness and interregionalism together is the fact that, when regions assume actorness, a need will necessarily also arise for more organised contacts between the regions, i.e., interregionalism.

A host of other intriguing questions unfolds as one starts to think about this general purpose. Is it plausible to speak of an EU foreign policy 'doctrine' of interregionalism at all? Is interregionalism really a crucial ingredient of the EU's foreign policy? Is the EU pursuing interregionalism only towards particular regions and not towards others? Is interregionalism more prevalent in some sectors and aspects of foreign policy than in others? In order to understand interregionalism we must, of course, look beyond the EU itself. To what extent does interregionalism depend on the counterpart 'region' and, particularly, its coherence?

A crucial question is to understand and explain why (or why not) interregionalism is being pursued. What are the interests and motives that make interregionalism happen? Does interregionalism occur as a result of power politics and geo–strategic (self–)interest? Or should we understand it as resulting from the effort to build a more 'just' world on the basis of core liberal internationalist values and ideas, such as democracy, development and human rights, which are often stated in the EU's official rhetoric? Or should interregionalism perhaps be explained in terms of social constructivism where norms and identities are seen as crucial components in the making of foreign policy and region–to–region relations? If so, then we can expect interregionalism to result from the projection of the EU's self on the other, or from EU attempts to act as a role model (or counter–model) for other regions.

Closely related to this question is another: who are the driving actors in the EU's foreign policy process and in the proposed interregionalism? Are they the EU's central institutions, national actors, policy experts, or perhaps non–state actors and interest groups? Of particular theoretical significance is the question whether the EU's foreign policy is a reflection of the so–called 'community interest' or intergovernmental bargaining, or just another means for pursuing conventional national foreign policy interests. Another way to frame this question is to ask where power lies in the making of the EU's foreign policy.

Assessing interregionalism raises important questions regarding world order and global governance. What are the implications of interregionalism for the patterns of foreign policy and world order? Does the EU try to construct regions and interregional partnerships in order to deal with regions through interregionalism, rather than the old–style (bilateral) state–to–state foreign policy relations? Does interregionalism imply a shift from a world order based on nation–states towards one based on regions and interregional relations? How does interregionalism relate to bilateralism? Does the EU have suitable partners to engage in interregional relations? Is interregionalism challenging or strengthening multilateralism?

These questions are both comprehensive and complex. Our starting position is that no single theory can provide satisfactory answers to all the questions. There is a host of different theories and approaches that are helpful in explaining and understanding European integration and the EU's foreign policies. To some extent we can expect that the dominant theoretical frameworks, such as realism and liberalism, will make sense of these issues. However, we can also expect constructivism and more critical theoretical perspectives to provide complementary answers, for instance on the role of norms, identities and power relations in these processes. There is a need to clarify, revise and also, to some extent, to generate new theory in order to make sense of the interregional phenomenon, as well as the EU as a global actor. Since the study of interregionalism is at such an early stage of develop-ment we have not tried to impose a single or uniform theoretical framework for the individual case studies but, rather, tried to encourage the authors to engage in creative theorizing.

Several authors in this collection employ, in their own manner, a combi-nation of different theoretical approaches in their studies (often a combina-tion of realist and liberal perspectives). For instance, Farrell (EU–Africa) sets a realist against a liberal perspective, whereas Aggarwal and Fogarty (EU–North America) derive and test several hypotheses from complementary strands of liberal, realist and constructivist literature. Julie Gilson's study of EU–Asia relations is rather different, in that she consistently employs a social constructivist analysis.

3. The Emergence of Interregionalism: a Historical Perspective

In order to understand the present and the future we first need to briefly look into history. Most observers agree that the nation–state is the main constitu-tive element of the modern international political system. The Treaty of West-phalia (1648) is a significant turning point in history. It ended the Thirty Years War in Europe and marked the formal beginning of the nation–state and of what is often referred to as the Westphalian system. "It grew out of the power of the king, and resulted in the sovereign, territorial state, which in turn implied the end of local power, as well as continental all–European political and economic structures" (Hettne 2004, 2). In this system the nation–state is not only responsible for internal order and external defence, but also for the welfare of its citizens and their civic engagement. This system represents something deeper than simply a dominance of sovereign, territorial states in international relations.

The Westphalian order emerged in Europe, but has gradually expanded over the globe. The nation–states in the Westphalian system were certainly not isolated from the external world. A dense pattern of international cooperation and regimes emerged that governed the relations between states, such as air traffic control and trade. The point is that these relations were based on state–to–state relations and did not challenge, but strengthened, the Westphalian system as such.

Globalisation, the Nation–state and the Transformation of Westphalia[3]

Today the Westphalian system is challenged and transformed by a number of forces and developments but also, paradoxically, reinforced by them. The most important changes contributing to 'moving beyond Westphalia' are perhaps the changing nature of its constitutive unit, the sovereign state, in combination with what is conventionally referred to as globalisation.

Globalisation is an elusive concept that signifies an ongoing process of structural transformation with worldwide implications. At the heart of the phenomenon is an ever–changing pattern of relations in time and space, which is a consequence of a global intensification of political, economic, social and communication linkages that have fundamentally altered the nature of social interactions (Harvey 1990). The process of globalisation can be seen to have reached a qualitatively new stage in the post–Cold War era. Economic interdependence was made possible by the political stability after the Second World War and then increased during the Cold War. Since then, globalisation has further intensified, which further reinforces the transformation beyond Westphalia.

The idea of globalism has as its ideological core the growth of a world market, increasingly penetrating and dominating 'national' economies which, in the process, are bound to lose some of their 'nationness'. Globalists consider too much government to be a systemic fault. Good governance is thus defined as less government. In accepting this ideology, the state becomes the disciplining spokesman of global economic forces, rather than the protector against these forces, which is the classical task of mercantilist nation-building. This historical retreat from its Westphalian functions also implies a dramatically changed relationship between the state and civil society and, in particular a tendency for the state to become increasingly alienated from civil society. In this process of change, legitimacy, loyalty, identity, function and even sovereignty are transferred up or down in the system, to political entities other than the state — i.e., to macro–polities or micro–polities. This makes it necessary to transcend the conventional obsession with the nation-state as the dominant political unit in the global system and instead think in terms of a more complex, multilevel political structure, in which the state assumes different functions. In the era of globalisation, new, larger political structures beyond the 'state' are obviously needed. In fact, the resurrection of regionalism is intimately tied to the transformation of the nation–state as well as globalisation.

Regionalism and the Emergence of Interregionalism

Although interregionalism should be seen as a distinct phenomenon, it cannot be understood in total isolation from regionalism. With regard to the latter, it is commonplace to refer to successive waves of regionalism or regional integration. Many observers speak about two main 'waves' of regionalism: the processes emerging after the end of the Second World War and extending until the mid–1970s and those since the mid–1980s (Schulz *et al.* 2001).[4]

In order to avoid the confusion that often arises as a result of mixing temporal, empirical and theoretical notions of 'old' and 'new' regionalisms, we propose the term 'generations' of regionalism rather than 'waves'. The label 'generation' refers to empirical qualities and has nothing to do with the "theories of new regionalism" (Söderbaum 2004; Söderbaum & Shaw 2003).

Classifying as 'generations' helps to underline the possibility of co–existing patterns of regionalisms with different empirical qualities, while at the same time also acknowledging that some varieties of regionalism build upon previous 'generations'. The use of 'generations' enables us to avoid the often–used dichotomy between 'old' and 'new' regionalism and a strict temporal division of regionalism at different historical periods. In the authors' view we are still witnessing the birth of 'first generation' agreements, which develop and co–exist next to 'second' as well as the more recent 'third' generation regional constructions. For instance, many regional projects and regional organisations were initiated during the era of first generation regionalism and were then simply renewed or re–inaugurated (sometimes with a new name and sometimes with different members) in the 1980s and 1990s.

The 'first generation' of regionalism often had narrowly defined objectives, and focused first and foremost on trade (or security). An example is the European Economic Community. European economic integration triggered the creation of similar free trade areas and common markets in Africa, Asia and the Americas during the 1960s and early 1970s. Such 'first–generation' regional integration is still a booming phenomenon. According to Sampson, "As of March 2002, a total of 172 RTAs actively in force had been notified to the GATT or the WTO. ... If RTAs not (or not yet) notified are also taken into account, the total number in force rises to 243" (Sampson 2003: 6).[5] Although mainly economic in character, the original intentions behind first generation regional agreements may also be political. This was the case with the European Communities: the driving force between the idea of linking the economies of France and Germany was security and the prevention of war, but the tool to achieve these goals was economic integration.

The main characteristic of second–generation regionalism is that it is more complex, comprehensive and political than in the past (Schulz *et al.* 2001; Söderbaum & Shaw 2003). As pointed out by Hettne, it is a "multidimensional form of integration which includes economic, political, social and cultural aspects and thus goes far beyond the goal of creating region–based free trade regimes or security alliances. Rather, the political ambition of establishing regional coherence and identity seems to be of primary importance" (Hettne 1999, xvi). Second–generation regionalism is based on the close intersectoral connections, for instance that trade and the economy are not isolated from the rest of society. As a result, regionalism also encompasses non–economic matters such as justice, security, the environment, culture and identity. In second–generation regionalism the number, scope, and diversity of regional projects have grown significantly in most parts of the world and they are no longer simply replicas of the early European integration experience.

The emergence of 'second–generation' regionalism needs to be historically situated. Telò refers to this as "post–hegemonic regionalism", emerging within a new and more turbulent world order (Telò 2001). The collapse of the communist regimes not only ended the Cold War and produced an enormous geographical zone of political uncertainty and instability, it also had deep repercussions for the Westphalian system. While, until the end of the Cold War, regional cooperation was largely a hegemonically imposed phenomenon, it has gradually become propelled by internal factors. According to Telò, what we refer to as second–generation regionalism can be seen as an attempt by states to react to the complex impact of financial, technological and market globalisation on their traditional territorial state power by strengthening regional control when traditional centralised national sovereignty no longer functions, and to bargain collectively with external actors and regions.

The EU is perhaps the most developed example of second–generation regionalism. It is a political model that challenges conventional assumptions about governance and even sovereignty. In fact, second–generation regionalism in Europe and, to some extent, elsewhere in the world is related to a transformation of the nation–state and "the dispersion of authoritative decision–making across multiple territorial levels" (Hooghe & Marks 2001, xi). European integration is a "polity–creating process in which authority and policy–making influence are shared across multiple levels of government — subnational, national, and supranational" (Hooghe & Marks 2001, 2). The multilevel governance model increasingly makes sense of the EU and the European political landscape. The multilevel model reveals a shift of authority in several key areas of policy–making, from national states up to European–level institutions, and at the same time a decentralisation of political authority from the national level down to the subnational level of government.

States are continuing to play important roles in regionalism, but they are integrated within a more multi–tiered and multilevel governance system. Here, it is important to acknowledge that, whereas first–generation regionalism in the 1960s focused primarily upon regional trade integration and was, due to its state–centrism, consistent with the Westphalian order, many of the current patterns of regionalism are more multifaceted and complex, and therefore reinforce the transformation of the Westphalian system.

Second–generation regionalism is to some extent extroverted and linked with globalisation rather than introverted as was the case with first–generation regionalism. This is evident, among other things, in that second–generation projects are stepping stones to, rather than stumbling blocks for multilateral trade. Second–generation frameworks can often be understood in terms of 'open regionalism' because the most powerful states and agencies on the world scene enforce such 'openness' on weaker regions and countries regardless of whether this promotes economic development or not (and in sharp contrast to the history of western economic development). Nevertheless, even if many regions 'opened up' and have become 'extrovert' it is not until recently that they have begun to play a role on the international scene. If regions start to become international and global actors, this may have deep repercussions on world order and global governance.

In the authors' view we are now in the early stages of the development of third–generation regionalism, characterised by a much stronger external orientation of regions, in which regions begin to play a more important role world–wide and in extra–regional affairs on a series of fronts: (i) towards global international regimes and organisations; (ii) towards other regions; and (iii) towards individual countries in the rest of the world (Van Langenhove & Costea 2004). While in first and second–generation regionalism the focal area is primarily the region itself, third–generation regionalism also implies external operations that can span the whole world.

Third–generation regionalism has at least two main characteristics distinguishing it from previous generations. First, in third–generation regionalism the institutional environment for dealing with 'out of area' regional policies is more evident and stronger. As an example, the European Constitution which is temporarily postponed, would give the EU a legal personality and create the first ever regional organisation that has the jurisdiction to act as a supranational organisation within the framework of the United Nations. Second, in third–generation integration, regions become more proactive, engaging in interregional arrangements and agreements that can have effect on relations at the global level. Following a period dominated by the EU in this field, regional organisations from all continents (e.g., ASEAN, Mercosur, Southern African Development Community — SADC) have started to engage in the creation of interregional initiatives. Given the influence of globalisation, there is a rather thin line between second and third–generation regionalism. However, a major distinction lies in the fact that, while the previous generations were aimed at optimising economic and political processes for the regions as such, third–generation regionalism is, by design, oriented more externally and towards shaping global governance.

Interregionalism is no novelty. There are several examples of region–to–region relations between first generation regional arrangements. However, it is our argument that interregionalism is beginning to have deeper ramifications for world order. The differences between the generations of regionalism are not always crystal clear. However, we contend that interregionalism should *not* simply be understood within the framework of second–generation regionalism. As Gilson correctly points out, interregionalism tends misleadingly to be examined within regionalism, and "regarded simply as a stepping–stone or body of resistance to globalisation" (Gilson 2002, xii). Hence, interregionalism is a new level of interaction and a distinct phenomenon, which needs consideration in its own right.

4. Concepts

There is still no consensus on the main concepts in the study of regionalism, and there is even greater disagreement in the conceptualisation of interregionalism. This is because the research field is in the early stages of development and the research object is still unclear and shifting. The editors' strategy regarding conceptual elaboration is to state some overall definitions in order to give the authors the opportunity to further develop the concepts for their individual tasks, if and when this is necessary.

In the most general sense, interregionalism signifies the condition or process whereby two regions interact as regions. We want to problematise two aspects of this general definition, which both impact on the way we understand interregionalism: (i) the actors of interregionalism, and (ii) the delimitation and understanding of 'region'.

First, with regard to the actors, it should be noted that, in the general debate, interregionalism is often defined as cooperation between two specified regions composed of *states* within an interregional framework or a formal relationship. As a result interregionalism is often considered to be mainly a states–led or intergovernmental process. In the authors' view, states are certainly important and often also crucial actors of interregionalism, but interregionalism is not intergovernmental by definition. On the contrary, various types of non–state actors from the private sector and civil society (i.e., transnational actors) are often, one way or the other, involved in the process. Their engagement is sometimes referred to as "transregionalism".[6] We consider these non–state processes to be part of interregionalism in the general sense. In addition, due to the fact that states and non–state actors are often grouped in complex multi–actor networks and coalitions, it is not always fruitful to understand them as two isolated and separate spheres of actors.

The second aspect, how to delimit and analyse regions, is more complex. Aggarwal and Fogarty (in this collection) use the label "pure interregionalism" to signify when the EU has relations only with one distinct and formally organised counterpart region, for instance a free trade area or customs union, as exemplified by the EU's interregional free trade area with Mercosur. There are many instances when 'regions' are less 'coherent' and dispersed, but when the concept of interregionalism still makes sense. Under such circumstances it is fruitful to think in terms of types or degrees of interregionalism. Referring specifically to commercial relations, Aggarwal and Fogarty take the Lomé Convention as an example in which the EU has trade relations with a set of countries from other regions that are not grouped in their own customs union or free trade agreement. They refer to this as "hybrid interregionalism".[7] In its relationships with the ACP countries within the Cotonou Agreement the EU is trying to establish the much talked about Economic Partnership Agreements (EPAs) with geographically more focused sub–regional organisations of Africa, such as SADC. To the extent that the EPAs are being implemented, they represent a deepening from hybrid to pure interregionalism.

The much–discussed APEC (Asia–Pacific Economic Cooperation) involves at least two regions but the individual states negotiate bilaterally and not as regions. Due to its special characteristics, APEC is sometimes referred to as 'transregionalism', that is, a somewhat less coherent (i.e., diffuse) type of interregionalism. However, the bilateral negotiations within transregional arrangements should not draw attention away from the fact that these are taking place within a broader interregional framework. Nevertheless, as several studies in this collection will analyse, there is an intriguing relationship between bilateralism and interregionalism. Whereas bilateralism may be compatible with, or reinforce, interregionalism, at times the two processes may also compete.

Bilateralism can also be a means for regions (especially the EU) to be seen as particularly strong, and hence as an actor. If the EU is perceived as a partner in a bilateral relationship, it is, by definition, seen as an 'actor'. In this sense there is an overlap between bilateralism and interregionalism, since a bilateral relationship between two regions (as actors) leads to interregionalism. But it is still fruitful to problematise and focus on bilateralism as such.

In this context, it is particularly important to acknowledge that the EU can act as one collective regional actor in a bilateral relationship or, perhaps even more importantly, be seen as 'one' by outsiders, for instance, when signing a cooperation agreement or when disbursing aid. Therefore, the EU is the half of the 'bilateral' relationship with another actor (which may be a state or a region or multilateral institution). Obviously, there are many issues to explore regarding actorness, for instance how unified the policy–making process is within the EU, but this does not necessarily detract from the 'actorness' of the EU. There can be similar disagreements within states about policy processes, but even if states are not unified we do not dismiss them as actors.[8] Being a regional organisation or a 'region' does not equate to being an actor: some actor qualities must be evident. Actorness can be defined as the capacity of regions and regional organisations "to develop presence, to become identifiable, aggregate interests, formulate goals and policies, make and implement decisions" (Rüland 2002, 6).[9]

There is a final aspect to the way regions are considered and analysed, which impacts on how interregionalism is understood and defined. Frequently, especially in realist and liberal thinking, regions are taken as pre–given, defined in advance of research, and often seen as particular inter–state or policy–driven frameworks. Integral to this reasoning is the idea that regions are believed to exist 'out there', identifiable through material structures, regional organisations and rational regional actors (most often 'states'). This is a pragmatic analytical strategy, which makes the study of interregionalism rather easy. However, at least in the authors' opinion, it is equally relevant to see regions as social constructions. From this point of view, the puzzle is to explain the process through which regions are in the process of 'becoming' and are constructed/reconstructed by reflective actors, whereas the conventional emphasis is on a particular set of activities and flows within a pre–given regional framework. The constructivist approach necessarily results in a more open–ended interpretation of interregionalism. It implies, for instance, that, even if there is no formal regional organisation or grouping to relate to, it can still be fruitful to refer to a 'region' and, in consequence, one can also speak of interregionalism in this way.

5. Structure of the Collection

This collection contains five case studies that cover different aspects of the EU's foreign policies, external relations and development cooperation. The first one deals with the EU's interregional policy towards Africa. Mary Farrell argues that, the EU's partnership strategy and the Cotonou agreement reflect neoliberal goals and the extension of economic liberalisation in the self–interests of the EU, rather than the normative agenda so often stated in the official discourse. The so–called 'partnership' with Africa is extremely asymmetric and also risks splitting and fragmenting the ACP group, thereby limiting these countries' negotiating strength towards the EU as well as within the WTO. As with the EU's economic agenda, Farrell is sceptical concerning the underlying aim of the political dialogue pursued by the EU and the proclaimed concern for human rights, democracy promotion, and the rule of law. These issues are so closely linked to the economic liberalisation dimension as to suggest that their inclusion supports the objectives of economic liberalisation rather than any fundamental support for democratisation. According to Farrell, Africa is useful for its markets, natural resources and minerals, and the EU's interregionalism is not driven by the ideal and norm–laden values so often emphasised by political leaders and policy–makers.

In the second case study, Sebastian Santander deals with the EU's most important "strategic partnership" in Latin America, namely with the Southern Common Market (Mercosur). Santander explains that this partnership is based on political dialogue, cooperation and trade. He argues that the interregional partnership is *inter alia* designed in order to enhance the EU's own legitimacy and its role as a global actor. But it should also be understood as an element in the EU's strategy in the economic competition between Europe and the USA for the Southern Cone and the Americas as a whole. In fact, the 'partnership' between the EU and Mercosur is being pushed as a counterweight to the American strategic goals to create a hemispheric market through the Free Trade Area of the Americas (FTAA) by 2005, in which Mercosur will participate. Here, it is of particular interest to note that, whereas the EU provides support for institution–building and region–building in Mercosur, the US has frequently tried to destabilise and undermine the Mercosur framework.

Julie Gilson deals with a third case study involving the EU and East Asia. She focuses particularly on the Asia–Europe Meeting (ASEM) and the EU–ASEAN dialogue. Gilson's study examines and demonstrates how the EU utilises interregionalism as one mechanism for managing economic and political relations with a growing yet disparate region. Gilson addresses, in particular, issues about the formation of identity, the enduring discourse of the Cold War and the (Western) norms embedded in ASEM's institutional structures. It is also shown that ASEM represents an important space for the articulation of non–state actors.

Vinod Aggarwal and Edward Fogarty show, in the fourth case study, that the EU has developed a series of bilateral relationships with Canada, Mexico and the United States rather than genuine region–to–region links. In this sense, the analysis reveals the limits and obstacles to interregionalism in the EU's foreign policy. Aggarwal and Fogarty suggest that economic security competition appears to be the strongest factor mitigating against the formalisation of the EU–North American link. This is most interesting as the same factor is important in explaining the EU's interregional 'partnerships' with many other regions around the world. In addition, the authors argue that the extreme economic and political asymmetry among NAFTA members, and the American dislike of trade agreements, are the obstacles towards the development of interregionalism between the EU and North America.

In the last case study, Karen Smith argues that the EU's relations with Central and Eastern Europe are not an example of 'interregionalism', or bloc–to–bloc relations. The enlargement of the EU has been the dominating issue in this relationship and this has, in turn, inhibited the development of 'sub–regionalism' in Central and Eastern Europe as well as interregionalism. Smith analyses why this is the case, emphasising the tensions between 'bilateralism' and regionalism in the EU's relations with Central and Eastern Europe. More specifically, she stresses that the absence of interregionalism is due not just to resistance by the Central and Eastern European states, but also to the EU's incremental responses to the primarily political and security dilemmas posed by including/excluding countries from the EU. Smith shows that this has affected not only relations with the new member states, but continues to overshadow the EU's relations with other European states.

The concluding analysis, written jointly by the editors and Patrik Stålgren, draws heavily on the five previous case studies in order to provide a comparative assessment of the EU as a global actor, and to account for the variation in the policy of interregionalism across regions and sectors. It provides three partly overlapping and intersecting (empirically based) explanations of the EU's foreign policies: (i) promoting the liberal internationalist agenda; (ii) promoting the EU's identity as a global actor around the world; and (iii) promoting the EU's power and competitiveness. The authors conclude by discussing some elements of an emerging agenda for research on the EU's foreign policy and interregionalism.

Acknowledgement

The authors are grateful for financial support from the Swedish Institute of European Policy Studies (SIEPS).

Notes

1. Guy Verhofstadt, The Paradox of Anti–Globalisation, *The Guardian*, September 28 2001.
2. European Commission Development DG, The Cotonou Agreement. Part 3, Title I, Chapter 2. Available at: http://europa.eu.int/comm/development/body/cotonou/agreement/agr14_en. htm. Accessed 23 February 2005.
3. This section draws on Hettne & Söderbaum (1999), pp. 359–360.
4. Others perceive three distinct periods of regionalism, also including the period existing between the two world wars, see Telò (2001).
5. RTA: Regional Trading Arrangement; GATT: General Agreement on Tariffs and Trade; WTO: World Trade Organisation.
6. "Transregionalism as a concept can encompass a broader set of actor relationships than simply those among states. Any connection across regions — including transnational networks of corporate production or of nongovernmental organisations — that involves cooperation among any type of actors across two or more regions can in theory also be referred to as a type of transregionalism", Aggarwal & Fogarty (2004), p. 5.
7. Hänggi (2000), p. 7, has a different understanding of hybrid relationships, which "may come close to interregional relations in those cases where the single power has a dominant position in its own region (e.g., the United States in North America; India in South Asia). Furthermore, relations between regional groupings and single powers may constitute an important component of biregional

or transregional arrangements (e.g., EU–China/EU–Japan and ASEM). The EU and ASEAN are the only regional groupings, which have a tradition of external relations with single powers."
8.   Thanks to Karen Smith for emphasising this point.
9.   Also see Bretherton & Vogler (1999).

References

Aggarwal, V. K. & Fogarty E. A. (eds) (2004) *EU Trade Strategies: Between Regionalism and Globalism* (Basingstoke: Palgrave Macmillan).

Bretherton, C. & Vogler, J. (1999) *Europe as a Global Actor* (London: Routledge).

Edwards, G. & Regelsberger, E. (eds) (1990) *Europe's global links: the European Community and interregional cooperation* (London: Pinter Publishers).

European Commission Development DG (2000) The Cotonou Agreement. Part 3, Title I, Chapter 2. Available at: http://europa.eu.int/comm/development/body/cotonou/agreement/agr14_en.htm (accessed 23 February 2005).

European Commission DG External Relations (1996) Interregional Framework Cooperation Agreement, 19 March 96. Available at: http://europa.eu.int/comm/external_relations/mercosur/bacground_doc/fca96.htm, (accessed 23 February 2005).

Gilson, J. (2002) *Asia Meets Europe: Inter–Regionalism and the Asia–Europe Meeting* (Cheltenham: Edward Elgar).

Hettne, B. & Söderbaum, F., (1999) Towards Global Social Theory, *Journal of International Relations and Development* 2(4), pp. 358–368.

Hettne, B. (1999) The New Regionalism: A Prologue, in: B. Hettne, A. Inotai & O. Sunkel (eds) *Globalism and the New Regionalism* (Basingstoke: Macmillan), pp. xv–xxxi.

Hettne, B. (2004) Interregionalism and World Order, Paper presented at SGIR Fifth Pan–European International Relations Conference, The Hague, September 9–11.

Hettne, B. (2005) Reconstructing World Order, in M. Farrell, B. Hettne & L. van Langenhove (eds) *Global Politics of Regionalism* (London: Pluto Press) (at press).

Hooghe, L. & Marks, G. (2001) *Multi–level Governance and European Integration* (Lanham: Rowman and Littlefield).

Hänggi, H. (2000) Interregionalism: empirical and theoretical perspectives, Paper prepared for the workshop Dollars, Democracy and Trade: External Influence on Economic Integration in the Americas, Los Angeles, 18 May.

Harvey, D. (1990) *The condition of postmodernity: an enquiry into the origins of cultural change* (Cambridge: Blackwell).

European Commission (1996) Interregional Framework Cooperation Agreement between the European Community and its Member States, of the one part, and the Southern Common Market and its Party States, of the other part, Official Journal L 069, 19 March.

Rüland, J. (2002) Inter– and Transregionalism: Remarks on the State of the Art of a New Research Agenda, *National Europe Centre Paper No. 35*, Paper prepared for the Workshop on Asia–Pacific Studies in Australia and Europe: A Research Agenda for the Future, Australian National University, 5–6 July.

Sampson, G. P. (2003) Introduction, in: G. P. Sampson & S. Woolcock (eds) *Regionalism, Multilateralism, and Economic Integration* (Tokyo: UNU Press), pp. 3–17.

Schulz, M., Söderbaum, F. & Öjendal, J. (eds) (2001) *Regionalization in a Globalizing World. A Comparative Perspective on Forms, Actors and Processes* (London: Zed Books).

Söderbaum, F. (2004) *The Political Economy of Regionalism: The Case of Southern Africa* (Basingstoke: Palgrave Macmillan).

Söderbaum, F. & Shaw, T. M. (eds) (2003) *Theories of New Regionalism. A Palgrave Reader* (Basingstoke: Palgrave Macmillan).

Telò, M. (ed.) (2001) *European Union and New Regionalism. Regional Actors and Global Governance in a Post–hegemonic Era* (Aldershot: Ashgate).

Van Langenhove, L. & Costea, A. C. (2004) Interregionalism and the Future of Multilateralism, Paper for the SGIR Fifth Pan–European International Relations Conference, The Hague, September 9–11.

A Triumph of Realism over Idealism? Cooperation Between the European Union and Africa

MARY FARRELL

1. Introduction

Relations between the European Union and Africa extend back far beyond the origins of the EU itself, and pre–date the institutionalised framework for cooperation that the two regions have built up over the past three decades. Nowadays, these relations are conducted under the auspices of the Cotonou Agreement, signed in 2000, and the successor to the series of Lomé Agreements that spanned the period from 1975 to the eventual agreement on a new framework. While containing elements of the practice, and some of the philosophy of the earlier agreements, the Cotonou Agreement has been hailed as a new departure in terms of both its substance and approach to Africa–EU relations. Broader in scope than the original agreements, it does retain the concept of partnership that, in the early 1970s, was considered innovative in the conduct of North–South relations. This notion of partnership is still fundamental to Africa–EU relations and has in fact been given stronger emphasis in the current agreement.

Even today, international cooperation among states and/or between regions tends to be explained through one or other of the interpretative lenses available within international relations theory. Different interpretations of the nature of the international system, and the behaviour of individual states within that system are key questions. Realism (and its variants) consider states as the key actor, in pursuit of self–interest, and the defence of the national interest, averse to international cooperation except as a second–best option. Liberalism (and its variants) enshrined the virtues of freedom and rejected the notion that conflict was inherent in the human condition, advocating the view that institutions can promote a Kantian international order based upon peace and justice. Idealism was even more strongly of the view that an international order should be the goal, built around normative thinking, for building peace and making a better world through international institutions and frameworks with explicit and implicit value–laden agendas (e.g., Baylis & Smith 2001; Jackson & Sørensen 2003).

Where does the contemporary framework for EU–Africa cooperation fit into this kaleidoscope of approaches to international relations? It is difficult to find much reference to the concept of partnership in any of the main theoretical approaches, much less to find a useful definition of the term in any of the explanations of international cooperation on offer in contemporary literature. Turning to the European Union, itself the architect of the 'partnership model', one is struck by the lack of definitional clarity in the various policy papers of the European Commission on the one hand, and by the diversity of partnership arrangements that operate in practice with other regions of the world.

Even a cursory glance through European Commission publications and the various country and regional strategy papers produced over the past three years reveals the extent to which such normative values as democracy, human rights, and the rule of law appear as fundamental principles and often key conditions in the development of substantive cooperation between the European Union and its respective partner(s). Implicit in this approach to international politics is the view that cooperation is necessary and desirable not merely in the pursuit of self–interest but as part of a wider agenda for peace, justice and equality, where power and politics are supplanted by an institutionalised framework to support dialogue and enhance the achievement of core values, including democracy and the rule of law.

How does the EU model of partnership work out in practice? To what extent does this institutionalised form of interregional cooperation reflect the core values that the EU claims to espouse and, equally important, are these values shared by the other partner? The real measure of success for any political partnership is the extent to which substantive outcomes can be measured against the aspirations of each party. However, the introduction of the partnership concept brings an added dimension for it suggests free will, equal weight in terms of influence and ability to shape negotiations and outcomes, and the expectation of favourable results for each partner. When cooperation is conducted through formal, institutionalised channels over a long period of time, rather than as a result of *ad hoc* and informal arrangements, the possibility exists of reinforcing mutual understanding, establishing credibility and certainty in respective policy initiatives and proposals, and reassuring the participating countries that common interests can be maintained and continually reinforced through collaboration.

There is a broader question to be considered here, and this relates to the nature of the European Union as an international actor. Recent events on the world stage have thrown into sharp relief the apparent differences between the US approach to international cooperation, and its reliance upon military power and the creation of *ad hoc* coalitions of the willing to support international policy. By contrast, the European Union represents itself as the supporter of a world order based upon the rule of law, where multilateralism rather than unilateralism is the driving force behind collective actions to solve common problems and resolve disputes. In contrast to the hard power which is the basis of US influence, the European Union favours the use of soft power in order to exert influence on the international stage, with an agenda that is considered much more normative in tone. Indeed, the normative aspects of EU foreign policy seem to be extending across its relations with almost every country and region of the world.

How does this image square up with the reality of EU–Africa relations? EU–Africa relations have long been characterised by an institutionalised framework for cooperation.[1] The Lomé agreements brought together seventy–eight countries in Africa, the Caribbean and the Pacific (ACP) with the member states of the European Union in a privileged relationship which allowed the ACP group to sell their primary products in the European Union market without the requirement of granting reciprocal market access in return. The original partnership arrangement implicit in the Lomé accords was substantially modified through the Cotonou Agreement signed by the EU and the ACP states in 2000.

The new millennium has brought in a new era in relations between the EU and Africa. This study will attempt to define the cooperation between the two regions, and to elaborate on the evolving partnership between the world's poorest continent and one of the leading economic powers in the contemporary global economy. The major contention of this analysis is that EU–Africa relations have, from the beginning, been characterised by the realist tendencies of individual European states and that, under the current EU policy, similar tendencies are driving the proposals of the Cotonou Agreement with the on–going negotiations on economic partnership agreements between the European Commission and groups of countries within the ACP bloc (see Tanner 2004). The earlier phase of EU–Africa relations was initiated because certain member states wished to retain formal links with former colonial dependencies in order to ensure continued access to raw materials and natural resources, and to protect economic investments already made or bring contemplated in what were now newly independent states.[2] The contemporary phase of EU–Africa relations reflects both continuity and discontinuity with former policy and practice.

There is continuity in the desire to keep market access and to prise open new markets through the negotiation of regional economic integration agreements between the EU and selected ACP states on the one hand, and the encouragement of regional economic integration among the countries of the ACP bloc on the other. Yet, contemporary policy goes further than the Lomé accords did to promote economic liberalisation and impose greater conditionality on the partners through the demands for reciprocity of market access, plus the requirement that the regional integration/economic liberalisation agreements should conform to the WTO rules on trade liberalisation.

Certainly, regional integration has become a major plank of EU external relations policy but, as the case of EU–Africa relations demonstrates, the EU is promoting a model of regional integration that is far removed from the model of regional integration that has evolved within the EU itself. In fact, what the EU is promoting is a model of economic liberalisation across the African continent and, in the process, attempting to secure for itself continued market access and privileged economic status in the continent's emerging markets. However, the European policy is much less active in addressing the real problems of poverty and instability that are likely to place severe limitations on either achieving economic liberalisation or securing broad-based societal benefits in the long term.

To support these claims, the arguments are developed in the following sections. The first deals with the early phase of EU–Africa relations with a brief examination of the Lomé agreements, and reviews the broad outcomes of this first experiment at a European–African partnership in a post–colonial world. The second section examines the shift in the European approach, epitomised in the espousal of the economic partnership agreements that were first proposed through the Cotonou Agreement. The European Union's approach towards the more normative elements that are generally attributable to the European stance in international affairs is considered briefly — focusing particularly upon democratisation. In Africa, the end of colonialism failed to bring peace and prosperity, and many countries continue to battle with war and internal instability while weak and failing states have constrained the path to full democracy.[3] Nonetheless, support for regional integration remains strong and has even shown signs of renewed vigour. The final section considers whether and to what extent the current model of EU–Africa relations is supportive of the renewed regional integration efforts at continental and sub–regional levels across the African continent. The question is of particular relevance since the constitutive treaty of the African Union proposes a form of regional integration that is closely modelled upon that of the European Union.

2. From Independence to Lomé

The origins of European relations with the countries of Africa and the Caribbean can be found in the historical ties between them, based largely upon the legacy of colonialism. Through the Yaoundé Convention of the 1960s and the successor Lomé agreements, the European countries sought to retain the economic links, the access to natural resources and raw materials and other strategic economic interests they had enjoyed under colonialism (Holland 2002). From the beginning, the then European Community built relations with Africa and the Caribbean around a set of institutionalised arrangements based upon the concept of partnership.

Not surprisingly, the Lomé Convention was hailed as an innovative arrangement for the conduct of North–South relations, and the management of political dialogue among countries with an extreme asymmetrical distribution of power. Of course, it evolved over time as successive accords were signed by the participating states to create an institutional framework for regular dialogue between the political representatives of the two regions, ultimately through five different joint EU–ACP institutions. Decision-making authority lay with the ACP–EU Council of Ministers, while day–to-day matters were addressed by the ACP–EU Committee of Ambassadors. Three other institutions completed the structure upon which partnership was based. The ACP–EU Joint Assembly, comprising representatives from the ACP States and an equal number of representatives from the European Parliament allowed for a democratic forum where views were exchanged, interests defended and opposing perspectives laid open for discussion. In addition, two technical institutions — the Technical Centre for Agricultural and Rural Cooperation and the Centre for the Development of Industry — were intended to support the development of the agricultural and industrial sectors in the ACP countries (Ravenhill 2004).

Building upon the colonial legacy, provisions for EU–Africa relations can be found in a number of Treaty of Rome clauses, including the Treaty's articles 131 and 136, which allowed for the inclusion of the then colonies of the six founder members in the customs union. Following the granting of independence, the new states were granted preferential access to the common market under the Yaoundé Convention. The Lomé Convention of 1975 was represented as the successor to Yaoundé, offering market access, without the requirement of reciprocity, to the primary products originating in the ACP group.

As a preferential arrangement, the Lomé Convention offered the ACP countries the highest level of privileged access (i.e., lowest tariff rates) compared to the other preferential agreements between the EU and trading partners. Moreover, the political dimension with its provision for regular dialogue at the highest level made the agreement distinctive. While the first Lomé agreement related primarily to trade cooperation, subsequent agreements were broadened in scope to include clauses on such issues as human rights, the rule of law, economic, social and cultural rights, and good governance (Ravenhill 2004; Holland 2002).

While it is not within the scope of this study to attempt a comprehensive analysis of the successes and failures of the Lomé agreements, a couple of observations concerning the overall record of the agreements are in order. Despite the developmental orientation of the Lomé agreements, the ACP bloc failed to secure any noticeable increase in levels of development, and in many countries growth had collapsed below levels that had prevailed during the 1960s. By 2000, ACP countries' share of the EU market had declined to half the level of the 1970s, while imports from the EU continued to rise. The asymmetrical trading relationship was mirrored in the unbalanced nature of political dialogue between the two partner–regions. The ACP group never had the necessary political weight to exercise influence within the partnership, and their bargaining strength was clearly limited to what could be negotiated with the EU countries by appealing to the conscience of individual countries or by embarrassing the EU into extending the agreement. It was a relationship based less on partnership than on inequality and general institutional inertia, described by commentators as a form of collective clientelism.

3. Cotonou and Economic Liberalisation

From the beginning of the 1990s, pressures were mounting both within the European Union and at the global level to force a change in this traditional partnership. Within the EU, the strategic interests of the individual member states and the union as a whole had changed from those that motivated the original Lomé Convention almost thirty years earlier. New preferential arrangements were under consideration by the EU, and the geographic focus of its external relations was changing to encompass diverse areas — from Eastern Europe and the countries bordering the EU–25, south–east Europe, Asia (and especially China) and Latin America. The partnership with Africa no longer held the political salience of the past, and the EU's political priorities now lay closer to home. Unlike the previous consensus among member states on some form of partnership, the closing decade of the twentieth century was marked by disagreement among the EU member states over the nature and substance of any new agreement (Forwood 2001).

The decade also witnessed a shift in EU policy on development and aid, to reflect the belief that 'trade not aid' was the route towards development. Moreover, the EU had shifted its position towards the approach long adopted by the international institutions such as the World Bank and International Monetary Fund, with conditionality clauses attached to agreements on aid and trade–related development programmes. In 1999, an internal reorganisation of the European Commission meant that responsibilities for matters relating to ACP trade were moved from the Development Directorate to the Trade Directorate. For many European commercial interests, the Lomé Convention threatened to compromise their own special interests, and disputes over the protective regimes offered to such products as bananas, rum, sugar and cotton showed just how complex these commercial relations had become, and how difficult it was to disentangle the web of interests.

Perhaps the greatest pressure for a change in the EU–Africa partnership came from the World Trade Organisation (WTO), with a rules–based trading system supporting a global open trading order. The EU–ACP agreement clearly contravened the WTO rules, since it offered preferential access to selected countries and discriminated against non–signatories to the agreement — something that was acknowledged by the European Commission in its Green Paper on EU–ACP relations, published in 1996.

The Lomé trade preferences were contrary to the principle of multilateralism and the most–favoured nation clause embodied in the GATT/WTO agreement, which requires that any trade concession offered to one country should be extended automatically to all trading members of the WTO. The WTO Article XXIV is the exemption clause, which allows for regional trade agreements among a small group of countries under certain specified conditions — one condition being the requirement that the signatories to the agreement must agree to remove tariffs on trade covering substantially all goods.

The Cotonou Agreement was drawn up within the context of the pressures from the global trading system. Consequently, it contained an agreement on mutual trade liberalisation (dropping the non–reciprocity of the predecessor Lomé accords), with a proposal to establish regional economic integration agreements between the EU and groups of countries within the ACP, and also among countries of the ACP bloc. Several aspects of the Cotonou agreement are worthy of note, for they represent a departure from previous policy. One issue is the regional economic integration agreements (now known as Economic Partnership Agreements — EPAs), to be negotiated between the EU and groups of countries within the ACP bloc. The EPAs must be compatible with WTO rules, and this requires the commitment of the signatory states to ensure liberalisation of trade affecting substantially all products and services, and covering all sectors. The second aspect is the shift away from treating the ACP as a unified bloc, and instead resorting to negotiations with groups of countries with a view to creating regional economic agreements, while in addition not ruling out the pursuit of bilateral agreements (a case in point being the EU agreement with South Africa).

The Cotonou Agreement reasserts, at the rhetorical level, the principle of partnership as the defining element of EU–ACP relations.[4] In practice, however, the proposals focus upon groups within the ACP, thus making the latter effectively redundant and threatening its very existence.[5] EPA negotiations have already started, in some cases with regional groupings that do not constitute existing regional organisations in Africa. There is thus a threat to the existing sub–regional organisations that already operate across the African continent. Given the multiplicity of such existing groupings in Africa, and the overlapping membership of many countries in different organisations, the approach taken by the European Commission to the EPA negotiations is likely to exacerbate a situation that is already inchoate and fragmented. What is really needed is a recognition of the existing regional groupings, and a concerted and coherent programme to foster deeper integration among these regional organisations — one of the declared objectives of the African Union.

While the successive Lomé agreements were conducted for five years, with the Lomé IV Convention signed in 1990 to cover a ten–year period, the Cotonou Agreement departs from past practice to cover a twenty–year period from 2003. Significantly, it also reflects a departure from previous practice by emphasising the role of economic partnership agreements in facilitating the integration of African countries into the global economy. In effect, through this programme of Economic Partnership Agreements, the EU–Africa 'partnership' would secure what the preceding Lomé agreements had failed to do, namely to correct the marginalisation of Africa in the global economy. In essence, the European Commission's Green Paper on EU–ACP relations of 1996 had already hinted at how the European perspective on relations with Africa had shifted, and the EU responsibilities lay in "actively support[ing] the moves towards more openness that started when the Cold War came to an end in the second half of the 1980s and in particular help anchor the democratisation process, which is still precarious in many ACP countries" (European Commission 1996, iii).

The agreement strengthened such political dimensions as democratisation, human rights, and good governance — at least, at the level of rhetoric. However, as the Green Paper suggested, the EU demanded an increased level of commitment on the part of the African countries to push through institutional reforms and to implement policies in the economic, social and environmental arenas arising out of the undertakings agreed to at international conferences. In effect, the demands made by the European Union on its partners had strengthened — implicitly, the European Union was treating the African states as if these countries had the requisite capacity to implement such reforms and conduct policies with the same degree of effectiveness as Western states. However, the contemporary state system in Africa is not comparable to the 'Western' state in terms of sovereignty and legitimacy, stability and capacity to implement policies or control the distribution of resources. Yet, this is the implication behind the European Commission's requirements and the specific expectations directed at the African partners.

Even as the European Commission was undergoing its own review of the Lomé Convention, the European Union was already questioning whether the ACP should remain the relevant partner for the EU. By the time the Cotonou Agreement was signed in 2000, the answer to that question was already evident in the decision to establish agreements with groups of countries, rather than the ACP as a single unified bloc. There was already a significant shift in the geo–strategic interests of the EU as a whole, and Africa had fallen down the list of priorities for the Union and even for the individual member states.

Whose interests were served by this decision to continue the relationship? From the perspective of the European Union, the Cotonou Agreement and the policy activities that arose out of the agreement allow the European Union to protect European interests, while also facilitating a mini 'regime–change' in the African countries, in accordance with EU values and standards. Even if the outcome is not realised fully, the European Union has established the channels through which it can convey its values, priorities and even special interests. According to the Green Paper, the EU could support the partnership by focusing upon the areas in which it considered the Union to have competence and 'added value' — promoting the observance of human rights, support for regional organisations, improving capacity for economic and social–policy analysis, the working of the legal system, and competition rules.

The decision to revitalise the political dimension of EU–Africa relations was a recognition that, under the predecessor Lomé agreements, the partnership was showing signs of weakness, based in part on the credibility gap associated with presenting this as a partnership of equals when the reality showed the African countries to have institutional weaknesses and a dependence on aid, and an inability to withstand the conditionality demands now being imposed by the European Union (ODI 2003). It was hard to maintain the myth of equal partners, with every sign that the principle of partnership was being undermined by the weakness of the African states and the widening gap with the expectations of the European partner.

With the explicit acknowledgement of the expectations–capability gap (African capability and European expectations) the logical result, as far as the EU was concerned, was that a new partnership should reflect the different capabilities of the African states. Thus, the new framework of cooperation would incorporate an element of differentiation in the number and type of partners with whom to develop cooperative arrangements.

4. From Partnership to … What?

The Cotonou Agreement was presented in one sense as a renewal of a long–standing partnership between the European Union and the ACP group of countries. However, the European Commission's Green Paper, produced as part of the review of the programme, underscored the changed global context in which relations must be conducted. Consequently, the Agreement, when it came, brought some new elements to the cooperation. Issues such as human rights, democracy and the rule of law together with good governance had crept into earlier agreements, and were reinserted with greater vigour into the new agreement. This time, however, violations of these principles could lead to the suspension of cooperation (or of aid) under a non–execution clause that was inserted by the EU and against the wishes of the ACP states.[6]

Under the Cotonou Agreement, the joint Council of Ministers, on which all parties sit, acts as the governing council and also as a court of appeal in the case of allegations of violations of human rights, democratic principles or the rule of law. This framework has yet to be tested fully, but observers suggest that it has real potential (ODI 2003, 11). Despite the long existence of the EU–ACP partnership which one might expect to have created a degree of understanding and mutual trust, as befits a partnership, the negotiations over the Cotonou agreement showed just how asymmetrical this partnership really was.

Although both accepted the need to intensify the political dialogue, there was much disagreement over the substance of what should be included. The

EU's insistence on the inclusion of good governance in addition to the other clauses on law, human rights and democracy annoyed the ACP countries, many of whom who claimed that a good governance provision was superfluous since it was implicit in the other principles of democracy and the rule of law. In the end, the parties adopted two procedures, one for consultation and adoption of measures in case of violation of one of the 'essential elements' (human rights, democracy and rule of law) and another for the violation of the good governance fundamental element.

The Agreement extended the scope of the partners, opening up to new actors apart from the central governments, and including local and regional authorities and civil society as well as the private sector. Two of the central dimensions inherent in the Cotonou Agreement related to the political and economic arenas. As indicated above, the political dimension was located in the dialogue on a variety of issues, and the conduct of such dialogue through the established institutional framework. The economic dimension focused upon trade, and specifically the negotiation of Economic Partnership Agreements. Art 35.2 specified the approach to be taken: "Economic and trade cooperation shall build on regional integration initiatives ... a key instrument in the integration of ACP countries in the world economy". Article 29 promotes regional economic integration, while article 30 advocates functional regional cooperation in such areas as infrastructure, water resources, health and education (European Commission Development DG 2000).

Several observations arise from this brief review of the Cotonou Agreement. For one thing, the outcome appears to reflect less of the consensual tone one might expect from a partnership, particularly given the fact that the European Union was able to impose certain conditions upon its erstwhile partner that the latter was unable to refuse due to asymmetric bargaining strengths. The second point relates to the much–enhanced profile given to the economic dimension, particularly through the support for regional integration. However, a look at the detail of the proposed Economic Partnership Agreements raises the question what form of regional integration is being proposed. Whose model of regional integration is under construction through the Cotonou Agreement, and how does this relate to what is actually happening with respect to the visions and programmes for regional integration in Africa?

The third point relates to the pronounced role given to political dialogue and, in particular, to the promotion of democracy. Again, the sceptic might be inclined to raise several questions concerning the coherence of the approach to democracy promotion, and to the overall scope of democracy enhancing measures by the European Union. If we have learned nothing else from the recent US war with Iraq, at least it must be patently clear that democracy cannot be constructed overnight nor can it be imposed from outside. As in the case of Iraq, we can ask 'whose model of democracy?' and 'how might it work in practice?' The next two sections will consider the coherence of the EU regional integration proposals which contrast with the renewed vigour for regional integration on the African continent, and then go on to reflect upon the rationale and logic of the EU democracy–promotion clauses in the Cotonou Agreement.

5. Whose Model of Regional Integration?

The concept of regional integration has existed in Africa ever since independence, and was best embodied in the ideas of pan–African unity that were promoted by some of the leaders of the newly–independent states, most notably by Kwame Nkrumah of Ghana. While regional integration receded somewhat during the 1970s, a variety of sub–continental regional organisations began to merge, largely based around the objective of development through regional cooperation.

However, despite the early high–level commitment and burgeoning initiatives, regional integration failed to achieve any measurable impact either on development or in terms of institutional structures or political outcomes. A variety of reasons have been put forward as explanations, including the lack of political will, inadequate financial resources, the various outbreaks of internal conflict which contributed to regional instability and the endemic poverty in many countries which left them deprived of resources to devote to regional (international) initiatives (UNECA 2004).

The situation began to change at the close of the twentieth century, and a renewed interest in regional integration brought the collective efforts of the African governments to establish the African Union (AU) in 2002, as successor to the Organisation of African Unity (1962), and the announcement of the New Partnership for Africa's Development (NEPAD).[7] While these are two separate initiatives, the NEPAD framework will operate with the approval of the AU. The real significance of these two initiatives is the strategic vision of regional integration that they offer, and one that is African in design and ownership (Herbst & Mills 2003).

Reading the Constitutive Act of the African Union, one is struck by the scope of the institutional and political structures as well as the objectives that are proposed. The AU will have an extensive institutional structure, including an assembly in the form of a pan–African Parliament, a Commission, Executive Council of Ministers, Permanent Representatives Committee, a Court of Justice, a Peace and Security Council, Financial Institutions (to include eventually an African Central Bank, African Monetary Fund, and African Investment Bank) as well as a number of lesser supranational entities. Plans are already under way to put these institutions into operation and the members of the Commission have already been appointed.

Contained within the Constitutive Act of the African Union are the key ideas concerning continental unity. Three of these ideas will be mentioned here, since they serve to highlight the vision of regional integration. First, political integration should be the *raison d'être* of the AU, the objective being to achieve a United States of Africa in the long run. This raises the question as to which method to adopt in order to bring this about — a 'big–bang' approach, limited intergovernmental cooperation, or building upon the foundations of the existing regional groupings. It was the latter approach that the AU members elected to adopt in the process of securing continental unity.

Second, the integration process should be geared to stimulating and re-energising the role of the states. This is both a practical and a political matter, for the African states guard their sovereignty with the same ferocity as do states elsewhere in the world (a notable case being the member states of ASEAN — Association of Southeast Asian Nations), even when the level of poverty and lack of development would indicate limited and, even, non–existent sovereignty in practice. Their support for regional integration is, therefore predicated upon the reassurance that national sovereignty will be respected and reinforced through integration, rather than restricted or eroded.

Third, regional integration processes should incorporate the interests not only of government representatives, but also those of parliamentarians, political parties, economic actors, and civil society representatives. Above all, the AU would proceed along the path of unity with integration at variable speed. This approach towards regional integration was clearly accepted by the African leaders meeting at the AU summit in July 2004.

The plan of African unity set out in the Constitutive Act of the African Union, and elaborated in the Strategic Plan of the AU Commission, is visionary. While Africa has never been short of either visionary leaders or visions, often the visions have been unrealistic and, in some cases, unasked for, while the visionary leaders either failed to realize the vision with the support of their people, or else proved to be self–serving autocratic despots. This time around, there is a common consensus shared by African leaders and their societies that underdevelopment and marginalisation requires a collective effort to generate a new development paradigm, with Africans at the centre of their own affairs.

The AU summit meeting held in July 2004 adopted a comprehensive Strategic Plan prepared by the AU Commission, agreed to locate the pan–African parliament in South Africa, and endorsed the progress made by NEPAD, particularly with regard to the implementation of the Peer Review Mechanism, which is already under way in several countries. The AU Commission Strategic Plan reflected the need to balance existing and future plans while bearing in mind the lessons of the past, stating "the stake for Africa is to formulate a home–grown development open to the whole world, rather than to promote an opening to the world which nips this very home–grown development in the bud".[8] The experience with Structural Adjustment Programmes in the 1980s showed how countries could follow the strictures on economic liberalisation without achieving economic development.

The regional integration model that is implied in the Constitutive Act of the African Union and the Strategic Plan by the AU Commission suggest a multi–layered and multi–faceted form of regional integration, incorporating political, economic and social forces, bringing in sub–national, national, sub–regional and regional levels of authority and decision making. It is a multi–level governance system in the making, yet it cannot, at this stage, be considered as arising out of a teleological process. The outcome is far from certain, and the actual progress towards regional integration will depend upon the coordination by the African Union, the political commitment of the individual African states, the leadership of the most advanced countries on the continent, and the extent of authority given to the regional organisations by the individual member states.

It is not the intention here to suggest that the plan for continental African unity is far advanced. As any seasoned analyst of regional integration will realize, the path of regional integration is fraught with difficulty and marked by many obstacles, so that forward movement is often accompanied by backward steps and reluctant partners who may determine the pace of cooperation against the rate of progress preferred by the more enthusiastic members. However, events can often take their own course, with unanticipated consequences for the processes of regional cooperation and integration.

This seems to have happened with the African Union's efforts to manage the conflict in the western Sudanese region of Darfur. Initially, the AU sent observers to the region, but the Sudanese government rejected the plan to send military personnel, saying that the government itself would take responsibility for the protection of all civilians within its national borders. Subsequently, it changed position as the circumstances in the region worsened, and international criticism eventually forced the government to relent and to allow an AU peace–keeping force to enter the country. In international relations, one successful cooperative initiative among sovereign states can provide the basis for further cooperation — and the AU's success in managing or diffusing conflict could enhance its legitimacy to act in peace–keeping and conflict management in other situations that arise, and increasingly on a continental (i.e., Africa–wide) basis.

6. Whose Democracy?

The preceding section highlighted the emerging vision of African regional integration. It suggests a model that bears many parallels to the European model, as defined in the Treaty of Rome, and that we have witnessed over the years as it evolved through the political processes and negotiations between the member states on the one hand, and between the member states and the supranational institutions on the other hand. While the African model still has some way to go to attain the level of maturity currently reflected in the European integration — and, indeed, there is no reason why it should follow that model precisely — the AU is undoubtedly seeking to construct a multi–level structure of continental cooperation. This is far more complex in design than the regional integration model that the Cotonou Agreement is seeking to impose on the ACP states.

The Cotonou Agreement also brought an enhanced dimension to the political dialogue between the European Union and the ACP group. As we have seen, this occurred through the inclusion of clauses on democracy, human rights and the rule of law. However, this was not an entirely new departure, for EU development policy had shifted in the 1990s, so that the promotion of democracy, good governance and the rule of law progressively became both an objective and a condition for EU development assistance (Santiso 2002). In fact, since 1995, a 'human rights clause' is standard for all EU treaties with third countries. The implication of this link to potential remedies in accordance with international law is that there is a greater possibility of some countries facing a suspension of aid.[9]

Prospective members of the European Union are required to meet conditions relating to democracy, human rights and the rule of law. Under the Copenhagen criteria, the new accession states were required to comply with these conditions before being granted access to the European Union — so they faced a dual set of challenges to qualify for membership: the adoption of the *acquis communautaire* and the requirement that they could prove themselves to be functioning democracies with legal institutions and adequate guarantees concerning the protection of human rights.[10]

Although the African countries are not applicants for EU membership, they are required to meet the same stringent conditions as the prospective candidates. This is certainly one effective way by which the EU can seek to impose its values upon other countries, and without the responsibilities that would normally be owed to new member states. However, for both applicant states and the non–applicant states alike, democracy is treated in an *ex ante* fashion; first, the country must comply with democracy requirements, then it receives the reward (accession for some, aid and financial assistance for others). In November 2000, the Council and the Commission adopted a joint statement to clarify the strategic thrust of the EU development policy. While poverty reduction would remain the main objective of development cooperation, it will only be sustained where there are functioning democracies and accountable governments.

This position taken by the EU authorities places an enormous burden upon poorer countries, with their combination of limited resources and institutional capacity (Babarinde 2004). However, it also raises questions about the nature of the democratic model that the EU can reasonably foster in any country under its focus, and about the ability of the European Union to promote democratisation. Democracy implies the freedom of the people in a country to determine who shall govern them, and how they wish to be governed. Moreover, as history has shown, democracy cannot be constructed overnight. It has taken many centuries for the Western model to evolve into what it is today — and even now it retains many imperfections.

It may indeed be the case that the European Commission recognizes some of the difficulties in the implementation by the African countries of this aspect of the Cotonou agreement (Krause 2004). Of course, democracy falls within the broad remit of the political dialogue, but there is scant attempt to define what is intended under the Cotonou provisions or through the subsequent dialogue, to identify what level or what scope of democracy is the focus of attention. In practice, the political regimes in contemporary Africa vary enormously, spanning a spectrum from autocratic dictatorship to elected governments seeking to improve democracy (Van de Walle 2001). Facing a diversity of democratic governance, from those countries with low levels of representation to those with stronger democratic systems, it becomes more difficult to assess a country's potential eligibility for assistance.

Even very recent history shows how difficult it can be to assess the true nature and depth of newly–formed or emerging democracies — one can think of Russia, for instance, or countries in Central Asia, without going further afield. On the surface, a country can exhibit the trappings of democracy, especially the more formal or highly visible forms — an elected leader, free elections, a parliamentary system. But democracy goes deeper than the surface institutions into the heart of the institutional system, to guarantee the rights of individuals, the protection of property, the right to freedom of speech, the protection of minorities and protection against the arbitrary use of power by the state (Krause 1998).

Can the international community assess the functioning of a given democracy, or judge how it might shape up in a particular country? The answer is important, for it is upon a careful assessment of the democratic potential that appropriate and effective strategies of support and assistance are based. In view of the double difficulty in this area — on the one hand, the legitimacy of 'imposing' democracy from outside and, on the other hand, the difficulty of making a correct assessment of the state of democratic governance — the international community has resorted to the use of both positive incentives and sanctions as a way of inducing leaders to democratize.

The EU approach is increasingly to rely upon incentive conditionality to complement positive measures of direct support. Under the EU–Africa dialogue, mechanisms have been established to support dialogue at regional (continental level), sub–regional and national levels, involving both political leaders and civil society. Regular assessments of developments concerning such issues as respect for human rights, democratic principles, the rule of law, and good governance are undertaken. With the first EU–Africa summit meeting in Cairo in 2000, the framework for inter–continental dialogue was established. However, after this auspicious beginning political problems hindered subsequent meetings. The second summit meeting, scheduled to take place in Lisbon in 2003, was cancelled by the EU due to opposition to the political regime of Robert Mugabe in Zimbabwe. Perhaps a stronger commitment on the part of the EU would have allowed the meeting to take place to allow engagement in the dialogue that was envisaged under the Cotonou Agreement, rather than to avoid the issues as a matter of political expediency.

How substantive is the EU's commitment to democracy promotion in Africa? Critics suggest the commitment is more rhetorical than substantive, in part due to bureaucratic inertia towards a long–standing institutional framework that many consider adequate for dialogue between the two regions (Crawford 2004). Besides, it can be easy for politicians to sign up to high–minded declarations on issues of human rights and democracy, and then forget about them. Declarations on human rights gain good press and publicity for the individual political leader in Western Europe at little cost, and there is not much danger of having an irate constituency or national interest group demanding that earlier promises are fulfilled.

Another reason to doubt the commitment/capacity of the EU lies in the fact that the strategic interests of the region have shifted in the post–Cold War era. EU strategic interests have shifted to Central and Eastern Europe, and to the countries of the Middle East and North Africa, rather than to sub–Saharan Africa. This means that sub–Saharan Africa has residual interest for the EU: concern with political stability, security and conflict manage-

ment does, in fact, impose on the political and other resources of the
European Union. But the undoubtedly more long–term project of democracy promotion in Africa could impose even more on the political and
financial resources of a Union not yet certain about its own immediate
future.

The EU policy towards sub–Saharan Africa is reactive rather than proactive, despite the strong rhetoric to be found in the policy statements
issued over the past decade. As the common positions and joint actions taken
by the European Union under its Common Foreign and Security policy show,
the EU is responding to situations of conflict and instability as they arise on
the African continent rather than working from a carefully–thought out strategic programme.[11] However, effective action is limited by the 'expectations–
capability' gap of the European Union, and the limitations imposed by the
absence of a common foreign policy which might allow the Union to speak
and act with one voice (Ginsberg 1999).

Just as we can question what form of regional integration the European
Union is seeking to promote in Africa, there is also the question of what form
(or forms) of democracy is (are) intended or foreseen by the actions and policy
statements of the European Union. Are democracy promotion and good
governance endpoints and outcomes in themselves, or simply means towards
securing and pushing ahead with economic liberalisation (Abrahamsen 2001;
Crawford 2004)?

The principles that lie behind the EPAs are imbued with the ideals of neo-
liberalism and the role that liberalisation can play in development. But any
consideration of how to link poverty reduction with development promotion
is absent from the equation, as well as the still pressing problem of settling
conflict and maintaining peace — all ultimately obstacles to economic
progress and growth.[12]

Even as the Structural Adjustment Programmes of an earlier era have
been questioned and challenged for their limited impact on development,
the underlying ideas of economic liberalisation remain; this time linked to
the political dimension introduced under the Cotonou Agreement. Market
freedom and political freedom (in the shape of liberal democracy) are
mutually interdependent, and essential to the achievement of developmental outcomes. Current orthodoxy suggests also that democratic politics and
a small–scale accountable public sector is both necessary and desirable for
an active free market. But in this perspective, the role of democracy
becomes limited to serving the needs of the market. This is not how or
why democracy was originally conceived, and is certainly far from the
conception of democracy so familiar to Western scholars, or ancient Greek
philosophers.

There are risks inherent in this new version of democracy, not least that
strengthening popular control over government decision making becomes
secondary to the demands of economic liberalisation. Even more problemat-
ical is the implicit (and often explicit) challenge to the power of the state in
the Cotonou Agreement. Development requires a strong state, and the
history of the advanced countries confirms the important role that the public

sector played in the allocation and redistribution of resources to support development and growth (Krause 1998; Schuurman 2000).

For the developmental state, the capacity to make independent decisions, to intervene in the economy, and to engage in regional cooperation where this is considered desirable by the elected government, are all fundamental prerequisites to fostering a real democratic state. This is especially true in the case of Africa, where the state system is still in the process of construction and development. In this context, a programme directed at democracy promotion would have more substantive and enduring effects were it to focus upon the foundations of any democracy — building the deliberative, legislative and executive capacity of the state institutions (Youngs 2001).

7. Conclusion

This analysis began with the suggestion that the EU policy towards Africa, as reflected in the recent Cotonou Agreement, is strongly realist in tone, and that the rhetoric on partnership reflects less a normative agenda than a trenchant pursuit of what are really neo–liberal goals and the extension of economic liberalisation in the interests of the EU. What is the evidence for this statement? For one thing, the provisions on trade cooperation and the promotion of economic partnership agreements lie fully within the scope of the WTO agenda, which the EU supports wholeheartedly. Nothing in the Cotonou agreement threatens the special interests within the EU (even when these are threatened by the broadening WTO agenda itself).

Liberalisation, privatisation, and support for the private sector are shared interests of both the EU and the WTO. By contrast, a large number of the ACP countries do not have private sectors with the capacity to withstand competitive pressures in the international market. Similarly, the requirement on all ACP countries to guarantee the protection of intellectual property rights, under the WTO Trade Related Intellectual Property Rights (TRIPS) agreement, imposes significant legal obligations upon developing and poorer countries, as well as depriving them of the possibility to benefit from new knowledge in the way that the developing countries did in the past (when the latter could copy technologies in advanced countries and adapt to suit their own level of technological development). The requirement for immediate liberalisation places restrictions on developing African countries, preventing them from extending protection to domestic infant industries against foreign competition, making it more difficult to maintain public services under national ownership, and restricting the opportunity to pursue industrial diversification strategies as part of a comprehensive programme for economic development.

Similarly, questions can be asked about the real aim of the political dialogue dimensions contained within the Cotonou Agreement. Doubts were raised concerning the normative issues of human rights, democracy promotion, and the rule of law. For one thing, these issues are so closely linked to the economic liberalisation dimension that their inclusion may appear to support the objectives of economic liberalisation more than any fundamental support for democratisation. The new partnership being proposed under the

EPAs marked a shift away from the cosy relationship of the past, and the groups of African countries could no longer consider themselves as equal negotiating partners with the European Union. Not only did the ACP bloc seem in real danger of fragmenting under the new proposals, it also would risk the loss to its joint negotiating capability in international organisations, especially the WTO.[13]

It has become clear that the partnership is what it had always been — an asymmetrical relationship between two groups with very unequal political and economic strength. The Cotonou conditions were largely imposed upon an unsuspecting weaker partner, and the inclusion of certain conditions exposed the latter to legal constraints beyond what might be reasonably anticipated in a partnership of equals (Arrighi 2002; Babarinde 2004).

A further consideration concerning the legal framework is that, while it offers a way of dealing with conflicts among the partners in the context of breaches of the Cotonou provisions and, in some sense, offers a way of trying to balance the asymmetric power relations, there are also concerns over the viability of this 'reciprocal accountability' arrangement. Clearly, the ACP group is the weaker partner even when it can act collectively. As the weaker partner, the ACP countries are also aid recipients, and benefit from trade and other preferences. This places them at a disadvantage in challenging the EU, potentially risking the loss of these aid flows and preferential agreements, and thus compromising their interests.

The question remains why this 'partnership' does not operate as a genuine alliance between the EU and Africa to change the nature of the multilateral trading system, and to band together so as to create a North–South negotiating bloc within the multilateral fora. That is how the idealist would view the strategic partnership. Yet, even the idealist recognizes that "the current neo–liberal hegemony of ideas sits broadly compatible with the self–interest of political elites and the outward–orientated fraction of the capitalist class in the EU member states" (Hurt 2003).

Strategic interests have indeed changed. Africa is useful for its markets, and its natural resources and minerals. But Europe's real prize lies not on the African continent, but in Asia, and specifically in China — where it is developing a new partnership, this time more evenly matched in both the economic and political dimensions.

Notes

1. For further detail on the historical development of EU–Africa institutionalised cooperation, see Lister (1997), and Mahler (1994).
2. See Ojo (1996) for a review of the changing relationship between the two regions.
3. The problems that many African countries experienced in the early phase of independence are well documented and, for good accounts, see Arrighi (2002); Faria (2004); Van den Walle (2001).
4. According to Kunibert Raffer (2001), the term partnership was mentioned 52 times in 100 Articles, and 9 times in the annexes.
5. This is also the view expressed in Hurt (2003).
6. Human rights, democracy and the rule of law were inserted as "essential elements" of the Cotonou agreement, effectively treating these as conditions that must be observed under international law. Violation of these conditions would open the way to possible remedies, in accordance with international

law, and having due regard to the nature of the violation. Under international law, any treaty party can suspend treaties if the partner commits a "material breach of the treaty" — this is provided for under the Vienna Convention of 1969.

7. For comment on the prospects of NEPAD, see Chabal (2002), and De Waal (2002).
8. See Commission of the African Union Strategic Plan 2004 1, 10.
9. There have already been cases of actions resulting from violations of these 'essential elements' — human rights, democracy, and the rule of law — when the EU adopted measures against Zimbabwe, Haiti, Fiji and Ivory Coast.
10. In fact, the democracy requirement goes back even further than the current phase of enlargement. In 1962, the European Parliament produced the Birkelbach Report which laid down the political conditions to be fulfilled by an applicant country. The existence of a democratic government was established as a precondition for membership and countries seeking to join the EC were required to recognize the principles for membership established by the Council of Europe: the rule of law, democracy, and respect for human rights and liberties. It was around this time, also, that Spain submitted an application for association status with the EC, although still under the non–democratic Franco rule.
11. For discussion of EU involvement in conflict management and peace keeping in Africa, see Faria (2004), and Wilken (2002).
12. For a critique of the limitations inherent in contemporary perspectives on development, see CIDSE (2003); Maxwell & Christiansen (2002); Schuurman (2000); Van der Hoeven (2000).
13. The EPAs were expected to be compatible with WTO rules on trade liberalisation, extending liberalisation on trade between the EU and the African countries to cover substantially all products, and dropping the non–reciprocal nature of previous agreements whereby ACP countries had free access to the European markets without being required to extend the same (reciprocal) access to the European producers.

References

Abrahamsen, R. (2000) *Disciplining Democracy: Development Discourse and Good Governance in Africa* (London: Zed Books).

African Union Secretariat (2004) Strategic Plan of the Commission of the African Union, Vols 1–3, Addis Ababa.

Arrighi, G. (2002) The African crisis: world systemic and regional aspects, *New Left Review* 15, pp. 5–36.

Babarinde, O. (2004) From Lomé to Cotonou: business as usual, *European Foreign Affairs Review*, 9(1), pp. 27–47.

Baylis, J. & Smith, S. (2001) *The Globalisation of World Politics*, 2nd edition (Oxford: Oxford University Press).

Braga de Macedo, J. (2002) Development Redux: Reflections for a New Paradigm, Paris, OECD Development Centre webdoc. no 3, available at: http://www.oecd.org/dataoecd/47/32/2765764.pdf (accessed 12 March 2005).

CIDSE (2003) From Cairo to Lisbon: The EU and Africa Working Together for a New Partnership, Brussels, CIDSE Caritas Europa and Pax Christi International, available at: www.cidse.org/en/pubs/index.html (accessed [date]).

Chabal, P. (1998) A few considerations on democracy in Africa, *International Affairs*, 74(2), pp. 289–303.

Chabal, P. (2002) The quest for good government in Africa: Is NEPAD the answer?, *International Affairs*, 78(3), pp. 447–462.

Clapham, C. (1998) Discerning the new Africa, *International Affairs*, 74(2), pp. 263–269.

Council of the European Union (2001) The European Community's Development Policy. Statement by the Council and the Commission, Brussels, 10 November 2001.

Crawford, G. (2001) Evaluating EU promotion of human rights, democracy and good governance: towards a participatory approach, European Development Policy Study Group Discussion Paper no. 20, University of Leeds.

Crawford, G. (2004) The European Union and democracy promotion in Africa: the case of Ghana, Paper prepared for the European Community Studies Association of South Africa's Conference on

'The Relationship between Africa and the European Union', University of the Western Cape, 22–23 January 2004.

Dannreuther, R. (2004) (ed.) *European Foreign and Security Policy. Towards a Neighbourhood Strategy* (London: Routledge).

De Waal, A. (2002) What's new in the "New partnership for Africa's Development"? *International Affairs*, 78(3), pp. 463–475.

European Commission (1996) Green Paper on Relations between the European Union and the ACP Countries on the Eve of the 21st Century: Challenges and Options for a New Partnership, Brussels, COM (96) 570.

European Commission (1998) Communication to the Council and Parliament on Democratisation, the Rule of Law, Respect for Human Rights and Good Governance: the Challenges of the Partnership between the European Union and the ACP states, COM (98) 146 final.

European Commission Development DG (2000) The Cotonou Agreement available at: http://europa.eu.int/comm/development/body/cotonou/agreement/agr 14_en.htm (accessed 23 February 2005)

European Commission (2003) Communication from the Commission to the Council, The EU–Africa dialogue, COM (2003) 316 final.

Faria, F. (2004) Crisis management in sub–Saharan Africa: The role of the European Union, Paris, Institute for Security Studies, Occasional Paper no 51.

Forje, J. W. (2004) Facing the challenges of globalisation and regional integration: problems and prospects for Africa at the dawn of the third millennium, *African Identities*, 2(1), pp. 7–35.

Forje, G. (2001) The road to Cotonou: Negotiating a successor to Lomé' *Journal of Common Market Studies*, 39(3), pp. 423–442.

Ginsberg, R.H. (1999) Conceptualising the European Union as an international actor: Narrowing the theoretical capability–expectations gap, *Journal of Common Market Studies*, 37(3), pp. 429–454.

Herbst, J. & Mills, G. (2003) The future of Africa: A new order in sight?, Adelphi Paper 361, Oxford University Press/ International Institute for Strategic Studies.

Holland, M. (2002) *The European Union and the Third World* (Basingstoke: Palgrave).

Hurt, S. R. (2003) Co–operation and coercion? The Cotonou Agreement between the European Union and ACP states and the end of the Lomé Convention, *Third World Quarterly*, 24(1), pp. 161–176.

Jackson, R. & Sørensen, G. (2003) *Introduction to International Relations* (Oxford: Oxford University Press).

Krause, K. (1998) Theorising security, state–formation and the 'Third World' in the post–Cold War world, *Review of International Studies*, 24(1), pp. 125–136.

Krause, A. (2004) The European Union's Africa Policy: The Commission as policy entrepreneur in the CFSP, *European Foreign Affairs Review*, 8(2), pp. 221–237.

Lister, M. (1997) *The European Union and the South* (London: Routledge).

Mahler, V. (1994) The Lomé Convention: Assessing a North–South institutional relationship, *Review of International Political Economy*, 1(2), pp. 233–256.

Maxwell, S. & Christiansen, K. (2002) "Negotiation as simultaneous equation": building a new partnership with Africa, *International Affairs*, 78(3), pp. 477–491.

Ng'ong'ola, C. (2000) Regional integration and trade liberalisation in the Southern African development community, *Journal of International Economic Law*, 2000, pp. 485–506.

ODI (2003) European Development Cooperation to 2010, ODI/ECDOM Working Paper.

Ojo, O. O. (1996) *Africa and Europe. The Changing Economic Relationship* (London: Zed Books).

Orbie, J. (2003) EU development policy integration and the Monterrey Process, A leading and benevolent identity? *European Foreign Affairs Review*, 8(3), pp. 395–415.

Raffer, K. (2001), Cotonou: Slowly undoing Lomé's concept of partnership, European Development Study Group Discussion Paper no. 21, University of Leeds.

Ravenhill, J. (2004) Back to the nest? Europe's relations with the African, Caribbean, and Pacific group of Countries, in V. K. Aggarwal & E. A. Fogarty (eds), *EU Trade Strategies. Between Regionalism and Globalism* (Basingstoke: Palgrave).

Santiso, C. (2002) The reform of EU development policy. Improving strategies for conflict prevention, democracy promotion and governance conditionality, CEPS Working Document No. 182. Available at: http://www.ceps.be (accessed 12 March 2005)

Schuurman, F.J. (2000) Paradigms lost, paradigms regained? Development studies in the twenty–first century, *Third World Quarterly*, 21(1), pp. 7–20.

Shaw, T.M. (2000) New regionalisms in Africa in the new millennium; Comparative perspectives on renaissance, realisms and/or regressions, *Third World Quarterly*, 5(3), pp. 399–414.

Stevenson, J. (2003), Africa's growing strategic resonance, *Survival*, 45(4), pp. 153–172.

Tanner, F. (2004) North Africa: Partnership, exceptionalism and neglect, in R. Dannreuter (ed.), *European Foreign and Security Policy: Towards a Neighbourhood Strategy* (London: Routledge).

Thompson, C. B. (2000) Regional challenges to globalisation: Perspectives from Southern Africa, *New Political Economy*, 5(1), pp. 41–57.

Van der Hoeven, R. (2000) "Assessing Aid" and Global Governance. Why poverty and redistribution objectives matter, Geneva, ILO Employment Strategy Department.

Van de Walle, N. (2001) *African Economies and the Politics of Permanent Crisis, 1979–1999* (Cambridge: Cambridge University Press).

Wilkin, P. (2002) Global poverty and orthodox security, *Third World Quarterly*, 23(4), pp. 633–645.

Youngs, R. (2001) Democracy Promotion: the Case of European Union Strategy, CEPS Working Document 167, October.

United Nations Economic Commission for Africa (2004) *Assessing Regional Integration in Africa* (Addis Ababa: ECA).

The European Partnership with Mercosur: a Relationship Based on Strategic and Neo–liberal Principles

SEBASTIAN SANTANDER

1. Introduction

New regionalism, as a trend, has been developing for more than fifteen years. Some of these regional spaces have reached a level of development that enables them to play a role on the global scene. This is the case for the European Union which, from the early 1990s, has deepened its institutional architecture and strengthened its international influence. Since the Treaty of Maastricht, the EU has adopted a new type of cooperation agreement in order to develop relations with third partners. These agreements have enabled the EU to negotiate region–to–region association with other regional groups. Questions of a political, security, cooperation, environmental and/or trade nature may be tackled within these frameworks. The relations developed with the Common Market of the South (*Comisión Sectorial para el Mercado Común del Sur* — Mercosur) perfectly illustrate the new wave of interregional arrangements that are emerging and shaping global governance. EU–Mercosur relations are based on three pillars: political dialogue, cooperation and trade.

With regard to the EU/Mercosur relations, different issues will be covered in this analysis. Do interregional arrangements enable the EU to increase its external action in 'low politics' and, if so, to what extent? What are the consequences of these interregional agreements for the new regional schemes such as Mercosur? By promoting interregional relations, is the EU becoming an 'external federator' for new regional experiences? In other words, are the new interregional arrangements only a corollary of new regionalism or might interregionalism also be considered a factor of consolidation for regional groups? Because interregional projects or agreements generally include fairly ambitious trade liberalisation agendas, the links between interregionalism and multilateralism are also assessed here. In the light of this case study, could we say that interregionalism arrangements, as well as regionalism, are undermining or encouraging economic multilateralism? By tackling this question, the analysis also focuses on the underlying ideology of new trends in regionalism and interregionalism.

2. The EU's International Role and New Regionalism in Latin America

The EU: an Emerging International Actor

The third summit between the heads of state and government of the European Union, Latin America and the Caribbean, in Guadalajara (Mexico) in May 2004, enabled the EU[1] to play a role for the first time on the international scene in its enlarged, 25–country, configuration. This summit was in line with the thinking associated with the 'Rio Process',[2] which, according to the Rio de Janeiro declaration of June 1999, aimed to achieve a "strategic biregional" (European Parliament 1999, 1) partnership between the EU and Latin America and the Caribbean, supported by a political dialogue as well as cooperation and trade. In so doing, the EU was gradually pursuing its strategy of *rapprochement* with Latin America and the Caribbean, a sub–continent that, for decades, has been subject to what could only be described as the discretionary domination of the US. At the same time, the EU reiterated its willingness to play a role on the world stage with a single voice, notwithstanding the intra–European divisions that arose just prior to the summit held after the 2003 Iraq war.

The Community's first attempts at *rapprochement* with some countries or regional groups in Latin America were made in the 1970s. However, it was not until the 1990s that the EU adopted a strategy for all of Latin America and the Caribbean (European Commission 1994a). This strategy of bringing together the two sides of the Atlantic was a European initiative, part of the change in the international context. With the end of the Cold War, the European Community — and Japan — began to emerge alongside the US as the new power centres in a world that was increasingly economically interdependent. This emergence of areas that had struggled to find their feet during the 1970s increased the competition among them and the US, helping to weaken the economic position of the US. At that time, the US economy was running out of steam, fuelling debate about its hegemonic decline (Telò 2001).

As globalisation accelerated, the Community's member states became more aware of the difficulties arising from globalisation, such as the ability to play an independent role internationally. The increase in globalisation — which, since the 1970s, has resulted in growing economic, financial and trade liberalisation worldwide — has greatly reinforced market ideologies. As a result, the concept of the welfare state has been vigorously questioned. There has also been a gradual dismantling of state barriers to the market economy and international capital movements (Santander 2000a).

The world's states and their economies have become increasingly open to the outside world, making them more interdependent and exposing them to more economic competition. One result, though to different degrees, is less effective national economic policies. This process, to which some states — following the example of the US, EU countries and Japan — have deliberately contributed more than others (Gill 1995), has weakened the power of the state. Yet the process has especially benefited the transnational economic actors that play on the same field as states or international bodies. Transnational enterprises have gained most from this change, acquiring more and more power to influence the domestic policies of states and the international relations process (Stopford & Strange 1991). This trend has also been facilitated by the development of new information technologies, which are structurally linked to deregulation (Telò 1998, 29).

It is against this background of accelerating global competition, states' weakened control over their national economies and the lack of satisfactory global structures that the development of regional structures has become more important in the eyes of states themselves (Gamble & Payne 1996, 251–252; Ténier 2003). The regional repositioning of states, in the late 1980s, gave rise to the new regionalism. Of course, there are many kinds of regional integration, which is why some prefer to speak of "new regionalisms" (Marchand *et al.* 1999). The unifying logic behind them varies widely from one regional organisation to another. Differences may depend on whether the organisations are pursuing a strictly trade objective, have common development policies, or bring together the countries of the North and/or the South (Santander 2004b). Some of these groups, taking their cue from Mercosur, were set up later. Others, such as the EU, were reinvigorated. In an unprecedented way, states — just like the US — were converted to the idea of regionalism.

However, the development of European regionalism from the mid–1980s transformed regionalism into an integration phenomenon without precedent, defying the pessimistic forecasts made by the realist scholars (Mearsheimer 1990, 199; Waltz 1993). From that moment on, the European bloc began to strengthen its internal structures and to adopt instruments consolidating its visibility and external action. The revival of European integration was part of the growing interdependence movement that resulted from globalisation and the new regionalist wave mentioned above. The end of the Cold War bipolar system offered the EU new international roles and a space to play them. The 1990s allowed the Union — whose activities internationally were no longer conditioned by bipolar rivalry — to embark on the "route of a clearer affirmation of its identity as an international actor" (Remacle 2000, 487). The member states focused on doing more than just the coordination foreseen under European Political Cooperation (EPC). Through the Maastricht Treaty, they gave themselves a Common Foreign and Security Policy (CFSP) allowing "the definition in the long term of a common defence policy, which would result, at the right time, in a common defence" (EU, *Selected instruments*). Moreover, the instrument of political dialogue[3] conducted with the external partners was strengthened. This initiative enabled the EU to present itself to others with a single voice and to make good and frequent contacts with third countries and regional groups, to establish links and exchange respective views on international issues.

However, following Europe's inability to move beyond a mainly declarative diplomacy when it came to acting with one voice and acting effectively in 'high politics' arenas — such as ethnic cleansing in the former Yugoslavia, genocide in Rwanda or the war in Iraq — serious doubts were expressed by the realist scholars about the EU's capacity to become a genuine international actor. By institutionalising the CFSP, the European heads of state and government raised expectations that they were not able to meet, due to a lack of compromise. This situation gave rise to the notion of a "capability–expectations gap" (Hill 1993). Believing that strategic issues are essentially based on post–bipolar international relations, the realist critics focus as much on the status of the EU as they do on its instruments for carrying out political and strategic actions. Since the EU is not a sovereign entity but more an entity subordinate to member states (it lacks a centralised decision-making authority and has no real military capacity of its own), it cannot really be seen as an international actor.

By concentrating on a state–centred and strategic conception, realist scholars reduce the EU's international sphere of activity to the CFSP (Petiteville 2002, 152–53) alone. Yet in other fields ('low politics'), such as foreign trade and cooperation with other countries or regional spaces, the Community has a genuinely influential role worldwide. In world trade, the EU has 20 per cent of the world's total volume of imports and exports, compared with 18 per cent for the US and 10 per cent for Japan. After more than forty years of trade integration, the Union now figures among the planet's leading trading powers. Given that the EU plays a crucial role in drawing up rules for trade multilateralism and globalisation in general, it has a genuine world leadership role to play in the WTO's trade negotiations (Smith & Woolcock 1999). That is because, with a few exceptions,[4] the

European Commission's mandate to negotiate is granted by the Council of Ministers with a qualified majority. The mandate empowers the Commission to draw up a proposal document, to defend member states' trade interests at the WTO and to routinely manage trade policy. European trade policy, therefore, acts as a real lever at the Community level. This policy has allowed the Union to simultaneously develop a network of new agreements — for economic cooperation, association or partnership — such as those negotiated or in the process of conclusion with countries or regional groups of Latin America.

Following the 1992 Treaty of Maastricht, the new cooperation programmes have included a chapter on political dialogue. Besides the 'traditional' chapters on cooperation (technical, economic, trade and/or assistance), these programmes also focus on policy that gives a major role to democratisation, human rights and democratic principles. Many Community cooperation agreements are now distinguished by their 'democratic principles' clause — setting a democratic conditionality — which could be interpreted as an increasing politicisation of economic cooperation (de Wilde d'Estmael 1998). To underline the Union's capacity for international action, we will look at the EU's interregionalist strategy with Mercosur.

The EU and Latin America: From 'Old' to 'New' Interregionalism

EU/Mercosur relations date from the signing of the Treaty of Asunción (1991), which created Mercosur (Argentina, Brazil, Paraguay and Uruguay). The Union was motivated to develop relations with the South American countries following their political, democratic and economic development. In the late 1980s, Argentina and Brazil moved beyond their long–standing rivalry for regional leadership and engaged in an unprecedented process of political and economic *rapprochement*, which served as a platform for Mercosur's creation.

The world's leading economic power centres took notice when the region became politically stable and began adopting competitive and outward–looking economic policies. They saw an opportunity for new outlets for their enterprises. The enthusiasm for this "emerging" (Sautter 1996) area owes much to the markets' unilateral openness policies. Other reasons include racing to privatise public enterprises, deregulation and liberalisation of economic activities, stabilising macro–economic policies to attract Foreign Direct Investment (FDI) and a far–reaching reform of the state. These policies coincided with the creation of Mercosur, which enabled member states to strengthen their neo–liberal reforms and which was a key part of their international economic policy (Cammack 1999, 103). With its 210 million inhabitants, a Gross Domestic Product (GDP) of 1,000 billion US dollars and very strong growth in its intraregional trade, Mercosur quickly became the world's fourth largest trading bloc — after the EU, the North American Free Trade Area (NAFTA) and Japan.

The development of Mercosur illustrates that current regional processes and globalisation are not mutually exclusive trends. By committing themselves to a regional initiative, states are obliged to introduce integration policies to increase the credibility of a region's members with external actors — among them potential investors. The conclusion of integration agreements with neighbouring countries obliges a state to exert greater control over its own economic policy, so as to compensate collectively at the regional scale for the loss of national autonomy. But because globalisation was a setback for all isolationist development strategies, the coming together of neo–liberal economic policies has greatly facilitated the postures of regional openness (Hettne 2001, 12; Petiteville 1997, 515). Thus, while globalisation is a series of processes and an ideology of economic management, regionalism must be seen as a manifestation of globalisation; the two developments reinforce one another (Higgott 1997, 280). Hence, it is more useful to talk of neo–regionalism than regionalism, when referring to the new regional organisations and the relaunch of old and now reinvigorated regional agreements (Santander 2000b).

Just like neo–regionalism, 'neo–interregionalism' is not a phenomenon in contradiction with globalisation: neo–interregionalism develops within and is constrained by the global political economy (Grugel 2002, 1). Both these phenomena have become characteristic elements of post–Cold War global governance at multiple levels. Neo–interregionalism is a corollary of the new regional agreements. However, as will be shown later, interregionalism can contribute to the consolidation of regionalism. Thus, there is a two–way relationship between regionalism and interregionalism.[5]

The relations between the EU and Mercosur are based on group–to–group dialogue. This kind of interregionalist initiative, first seen in the 1970s, was related to 'old' regionalism (Hänggi 2000, 4–5). It was the fruit of European Community action. With the Andean Pact, the Community supported the Latin American regional integration efforts.[6] Support was limited to trade and development cooperation. Inspired by its own integration model, the EU gradually realised that "subjects of a political nature, such as the prevention of conflicts and the war on drugs, could be tackled in a more appropriate way by increasing the efforts made at the regional level" (European Commission 1995a, 2). The creation of European Political Cooperation (EPC) facilitated the development of group–to–group political dialogue (Regelsberger 1998, 2).

A typical example of the 'old' interregionalism is the one the EC developed with the countries of the Central American Common Market (CACM).[7] The armed conflicts in Central America in the 1980s encouraged the EC to play a major political role as an international broker. The EC established the San José Dialogue with the countries of Central America. This dialogue involved ministerial meetings aimed at achieving peace and democratising the region. The European strategy was based on regular and institutionalised political dialogue, plus a strengthening of development cooperation and support for reinforcement of the regional space (Rubio 2004). However, the old interregionalism was both sporadic and rather limited by the bipolar international context.

With the end of the Cold War, increasing economic interdependence, the emergence of new regionalism and both the deepening of European integration and the adoption of new instruments to consolidate its external action (discussed earlier), the EU was able to develop a series of new and much more ambitious interregional agreements. These agreements included the group–to–group association that is being negotiated with Mercosur. The interregional agenda now include mutual trade–liberalisation programmes in keeping with the rules and disciplines of the international economic institutions, such as the WTO. These new programmes are even more ambitious than those at the multilateral level. The compatibility required between the WTO and any other kind of free trade agreement means there is less and less room in the interregional agreements for tradi-tional development cooperation policies, such as the Generalised System of Preferences (GSP) granted unilaterally by the EC to regional areas made up of developing countries such as the Andean Community (CAN) or the CACM. As a result, while neo–interregionalism includes strategic elements, it is distinguished by its neo–liberal economic leanings.

3. The EU Group–to–Group Strategy Towards Mercosur

Structure and Actors

Both the processes of democratisation and economic liberalisation which took place in the late 1980s in South America, as well as the emergence of new regionalism, were important factors for *rapprochement* with Europe, according to the European Commission (European Commission 1995b, 5–6). The Commission therefore developed a strategy to institution-alise the growing links between Europe and the countries that constitute Mercosur. 'Third–generation' agreements signed between 1990 and 1992 with each of the four countries of Mercosur replaced the 'empty–shell' agree-ments of the 1970s and 1980s and revitalised relations. The new agreements are notable for the interest paid to integration and regional cooperation. They are also unique for the inclusion of two clauses. The 'democratic principles' clause calls for respect to the basic principles that stem from a heritage of common values. The 'future developments' clause enables the contracting parties to complete and increase their level of cooperation, moving beyond trade alone (European Commission 1995b, 8).

Behind these new agreements is an EU eager to develop interregional group–to–group relations with Mercosur. The EU capitalised on the interest expressed by Mercosur members to sign an agreement for inter–institutional cooperation. The agreement's main goal was to allow Mercosur to benefit from European experience in regional integration, so Mercosur could even-tually become the Community's main partner in relations with the Southern Common Market countries. Following this, the EU began to offer assistance to Mercosur with technical norms, tariffs and agriculture.

The EU provides Mercosur's Secretariat with technical assistance in fields such as training, computer networks, documentation and archives. It also supports Mercosur presidencies in promotion activities such as seminars and conferences. Mercosur also benefits from a programme establishing a customs code, which has resulted in Europe–based training courses for customs officials, and missions by European experts to Mercosur customs administrations. Cooperation has also covered assistance from the European Standardisation Committee (CEN) in drawing up technical and quality standards (courses, international meetings, training and annual conferences), as well as help with agricultural projects (institutional aspects, veterinary and phytosanitary sectors). This cooperation has enabled the EU to export its regional governance model and to increase its reputation as an international actor (Santander 2001). Furthermore, the group–to–group strategy has encouraged the harmonisation of economic rules at the regional level so that Mercosur could create its own customs union. A union like this will allow European enterprises to trade freely (without customs barriers) and to enjoy economies of scale.[8]

European technical assistance provided to Mercosur, in addition to the accompanying political and institutional dialogue, proved essential during the period of uncertainty experienced by the South American bloc from 1992 to 1993. At that time, Brazil, led by President Collor, dealt with a serious economic, political and institutional crisis. Argentina, under President Menem, was dissociating itself from its Brazilian neighbour and warmly welcomed the offer from the US to join the group of negotiating countries in NAFTA. The US proposal endangered the objective that Mercosur member states had fixed for themselves under the 1991 Treaty of Asunción, namely the creation by 1995 of a common external tariff with a view to setting up a free trade area and a customs union. Throughout this period of uncertainty, the EU supported Mercosur and developed a substantial political and diplomatic dialogue with the organisation (Hillcoat 1997, 105).

The US proposal was in keeping with its dual–track strategy for trade liberalisation (Payne 1996). While pressing for progress in trade multilateralism, the US envisioned, in the transitional period between the bipolar and post–Cold War eras, a strategic network of regional, transregional and hybrid agreements.[9] The aim was to integrate all nations into a framework of norms and behaviour — a framework inspired by the United States. To that end, the US became actively involved in Asia–Pacific Economic Cooperation (APEC). In 1990 it launched the Enterprise for the Americas Initiative (EAI), to create a free trade area from Alaska in the north to Tierra del Fuego in the south. The EAI was followed by a hybrid agreement with the four countries of Mercosur under the name '4 + 1', then by NAFTA and the launch of the negotiations for the transregional free trade area of the Americas (FTAA). Contrary to the European vision, the US authorities consider that the Latin American regional spaces are merely temporary and must eventually be absorbed into the broader spaces proposed by the US (Bergsten 1996). The integrationist project under development in South America is viewed with suspicion by the US, as the project is a barrier to its pan–American free trade initiative. The US proposed that pro–American Argentina (then under Menem) should join its project, hoping this would destabilise Mercosur and gradually extend NAFTA to the rest of the Americas.

The EU was aware of the threat posed by the US project to its strategy of *rapprochement* with Asia, Latin America and, of course, Mercosur. In a European Commission communication, the EU revealed to what extent the signing of the trade agreements with third countries or groups is economically and strategically important for the Union:

> FTAs [free trade areas] are economically beneficial, especially where they help the EU to bolster its presence in the faster growing economies of the world, which is our overriding interest. ... This direct economic justification has also been supplemented by strategic considerations regarding the need to reinforce our presence in particular markets and to attenuate the potential threat of others establishing privileged relations with countries which are economically important to us (European Commission 1995c, 7).

The fear of being squeezed out of South America stimulated the EU to react, all the more so because, in capturing 60 per cent of the investments made by European enterprises in Latin America, Mercosur became a leading partner of the EU in the Latin American sub–continent (Giordano & Santiso 2000, 59). European Commissioner Manuel Marín, who had the Latin America portfolio under the Santer Commission, proposed that the economic and trade links be enhanced in two stages; first, through the setting up of an inter-regional agreement for economic and trade cooperation and second, through the implementation of an interregional association of a political and economic nature, aimed at encouraging interregional flows, promoting the strategy of investments by enterprises and reinforcing political cooperation at the international level through convergence of the positions of the EU and Mercosur in international bodies (European Commission 1994b).

By approving this strategy, the Essen European Council of December 1994 decided to set up "a new and extended partnership between the two regions" (European Council 1994, 16). In the same period, the four presidents of Mercosur member states meeting at the Ouro Preto summit (Brazil) approved this strategic move. On 22 December 1994 in Brussels, a "joint formal declaration of the Council of the European Union and the European Commission, on the one hand, and the member states of Mercosur, on the other hand" stipulated that the parties are committed to "concluding an interregional framework agreement concerning economic and trade cooperation" during 1995 and to "set up a closer political cooperation" (Official Journal of the Communities 1994, 1–2). The European Parliament (European Parliament 1995, 10) and the Economic and Social Committee (European Economic and Social Committee 1996, 135–140) supported the strengthening of relations between the EU and Mercosur. For the European Parliament, a *rapprochement* such as this preserved the EU's trade role and prevented the whole of the Latin American Southern Cone from falling under the US umbrella. Lastly, the Cannes European Council of June 1995 gave the Commission a mandate to complete the negotiations of an interregional framework agreement with Mercosur; Mercosur heads of state gathered in Asunción in August 1995 to confirm the mandate for negotiations.

At the Madrid European Council of December 1995, the Union and Mercosur signed the fourth–generation EU–Mercosur Interregional Framework for Cooperation Agreement (EMIFCA), which includes the democratic and future developments clauses of the third–generation agreements. By associating two customs unions, this agreement added something new to international relations. The signing of the framework agreement between two regions was only possible because Mercosur was given a legal status in international law, following a demand made by the EU. This status allowed it to sign international agreements and trade conventions. The hope of gaining access to the European market after the signing of a trade agreement with the Union boosted the development of Mercosur, dispelling the prospect of a weakened bloc in the continental liberalisation movement launched by the US. Thus there was confirmation of the theory that the EU has a role as an "external federator" (Rüland 2002a, 11) for new regional experiences, through its inter-regionalist projects.

The EMIFCA is based on three pillars. The first institutionalises a regular 'political dialogue' for bi–regional consultation and coordination of the partners' positions on multilateral questions in the international bodies. The second foresees cooperation in fields such as the war on drugs and its consequences, culture, information and communication, as well as training in regional integration with a focus on the social dimension. Mercosur has also requested that there be some cooperation on regional integration, to help the body benefit from European experience. The third and last pillar focuses on strengthening economic and commercial cooperation "which should include a liberalisation of all trade in goods and services, aiming at free trade, in conformity with WTO rules". For the EU, this type of agreement should act as a propellor for multilateral trade liberalisation, since the EU believes that "FTAs promote the principle of open regionalism and can generate trade liberalisation that subsequently spreads to the multilateral field" (European Commission 1995c, 7). In reality, the FTAs must be WTO–plus agreements. In other words, the trade negotiations at the interregional level should aim to achieve more than those at the multilateral level. In this way, by effectively supporting the economic and trade harmonisation of the other regional spaces and then signing interregional trade agreements with them, the EU seeks to drive forward the multilateral liberalisation programmes.

In this process of *rapprochement* between the EU and Mercosur, transnational companies started progressively and naturally to play a very dynamic role. In a very short time period, the flows of private capital and commercial trade increased exponentially, making Europe the leading investor and trading partner of the Southern Cone, ahead of the US. The Europeans became the principal investors in the South American countries. European enterprises are actively conquering the South American market, benefiting from the regional integration efforts and the privatisation and macro–economic stability policies that result from the Argentine convertibility plan (1991) and the plan Real in Brazil (1994) (both linking the national currency to the US dollar).

The most active investors in the Southern Cone are Spanish, German, French, Dutch and Italian firms. In the race to acquire markets, Spain has quickly moved to the head of the European group (ECLAC 2000). Argentina and Brazil now account for more than half of the European capital stock cumulated in Latin America. In Mercosur, 75 per cent of the flows go to Brazil and 24 per cent to Argentina, compared with just one per cent for Paraguay and Uruguay. The European investments are especially concentrated in the service sectors (financial, telecommunications), (Giordano & Santiso 2000, 59–66). Since the launch of Mercosur, the Southern Cone economies have become a magnet for European transnational companies' strategies. These strategies see the South American market as a new financial horizon, a way of opening up to global competition and staking the EU's place among competitors. For the EU, the relation with Mercosur is strategic. This is why European enterprises wanting to see a free trade agreement signed between the EU and Mercosur created a powerful lobby, Mercosur–European Business Forum (MEBF) in early 1999, with the support of the European Commission (European Commission's Enterprise Desk 2004b).

A business forum, whose influence springs from regular meetings organised by the negotiators, often accompanies the new trend of interregionalism. To increase their visibility, coordinate their position so as to better promote their interests and to apply pressure on the decision–makers (governments and supranational institutions), these enterprises link up in fora. They can then follow the negotiations and are well positioned to submit their proposals to working groups and policy–makers.

The European Commission neatly sums up this situation:

> These [Business Round Tables and Dialogues] are regular events which bring together private economic operators, providing opportunities for developing contacts and stable networks between top industry representatives on both sides, industrial organisations and government officials. The usual outcome of such international meetings is recommendations addressed to the EU and the respective governments on e.g. market access, trade policy and foreign direct investment issues. The European Commission, since the nineties, has sponsored industry–led Industrial Round Tables ... These Round Tables and Business Dialogues produce annual recommendations aiming at the improvement of the business environment. Follow–up and progress reports are used as instruments for efficient implementation of those recommendations on both sides (European Commission's Enterprise Desk 2004a).

There has been considerable growth in the trade of goods. From 1990 to 1998, EU exports to the South American bloc increased by 375 per cent, while the Community's share of exports from Mercosur rose from 14.4 per cent to 21.6 per cent during the same period, resulting in a major trade deficit for the Southern Cone economies (IRELA 1999a, 11–13). The rise in European exports to Mercosur countries was mainly the result of unilateral trade liberalisation policies adopted by the South American governments from the early 1990s. Because of the trade imbalance, however, the Southern Cone national economies became much more dependent on the European market than the EU became on Mercosur. So, in addition to the strong dependence of the South American economies on European capital, a trade dependence also developed. While the EU represents 26 per cent of Mercosur's external trade and thus became its leading trading partner, Mercosur only represents 2.9 per cent of EU external trade.

With regard to the structure of trade, the Southern Cone countries — although they have reduced the share of their raw materials exports to the European countries since the 1970s — continue to export a large volume of processed foodstuffs to this region. Some 51 per cent of EU imports are agricultural goods, while these products account for only 4.5 per cent of EU exports to Mercosur. 49 per cent of EU purchases are industrial goods, while 95.5 per cent of EU sales are industrial goods (Cienfuegos Mateo 2003, 262). Unlike the South American exports to the EU, the European exports are notable for their high added value. The trade structure between Mercosur and the EU bears a strong resemblance to North–South relations.

Internal Obstacles

The external trade structure of Mercosur and of the EU is, to some extent, complementary and favours trade *rapprochement* between the two parties. Nevertheless, South American agricultural exports to the European market face serious obstacles. First, there are numerous European non–tariff barriers. Among them are phytosanitary and antidumping measures that affect the products of key economic sectors in which the Mercosur countries have a comparative advantage. Mercosur countries find themselves competing unfairly for these products with European firms (IRELA 1999b, 6) because of trade barriers that serve to protect so–called 'sensitive' sectors, such as beef, cereals and sugar — sectors that are the subject of specific policies under the EU's Common Agricultural Policy (CAP), which aims to protect European agricultural production. Mercosur countries believe they are put at a particular disadvantage by the CAP which has led to a widening of the Mercosur trade deficit with the EU since 1995. This dossier has proved to be a major obstacle to the launch of negotiations for a trade association between the EU and Mercosur, an association foreseen at the first summit of the EU, Latin America and the Caribbean in June 1999.

To start talks with the South American bloc, the European Commission needed a negotiation mandate from the Council. But major differences arose among the Council's member states regarding the delivery of the negotiation mandate to the Commission, for it was established that a free trade area with Mercosur could seriously harm European agriculture. The majority of the ministers of industry, economics and foreign affairs from the EU member states appeared to support the negotiations with Mercosur. But the French, Irish and Dutch ministers of agriculture and fisheries, under pressure from their domestic lobbies, were opposed to this mandate (IRELA 1999a, 9).

The UK government was of the opinion that the negotiations with Mercosur should not begin before the end of the following WTO round. There was also disagreement in the Santer Commission (1995–1999). The Agriculture Commissioner Franz Fischler, supported by his colleagues from France (Commissioners de Silguy and Cresson) and Ireland (Flynn), also opposed the project. Further support for this position came from the European agricultural lobby COPA–COGECA,[10] which was against any kind of trade agreement with Mercosur (COPA 2004). Those opposed to trade liberalisation justified their position by underlining the 'multifunctional' nature of agriculture in Europe,[11] a position deemed by Mercosur countries to be a new way of delaying the negotiations. However, the project was supported by Commissioner Marín, the German presidency of the EU (in the first six months of 1999) and the Spanish, Italian and Portuguese governments, not to mention Mercosur–European Business Forum, which was set up specifically (in February 1999) to help the interregional negotiations through a daily dialogue between the entrepreneurs and public authorities of each region (European Commission' Mercosur Desk 2000, 4).

The compromise eventually achieved gave the Commission a mandate to start the negotiations on non–tariff barriers, but delayed any discussions on customs duties until July 2001. These discussions could not, at any rate, be completed before the end of the WTO round, allowing the EU to avoid tackling at the interregional level the question of subsidies for agricultural exports. In any case, as far as the Union is concerned, subjects like these must only be handled in negotiations within the WTO. The Commission, therefore, attended the EU–Mercosur summit (held alongside the Río summit) with a limited negotiating mandate. It took four years from the signing of the EU–Mercosur Interregional Framework for Cooperation Agreement (EMIFCA) for the representatives of the two regional blocs to build a picture of the trade situation and, not without some disappointments for Mercosur, to start negotiations on the non–tariff barriers alone. The negotiations were launched during the first meeting of the Biregional Cooperation Council (BCC), which defined the structure, methodology and schedule for the negotiations and created the Biregional Negotiations Committee (BNC). The committee, to which a Subcommittee on Cooperation (SCC), three Subgroups on specific cooperation areas and three Technical Groups (TG) dealing with trade matters are linked, has become the main body for negotiations between the EU and Mercosur,. The four first meetings of the BNC were limited to questions of methodology, exchange of information and analysis of the basic prerequisites for starting the tariff negotiations. No real progress was made, underlining deadlock in the relations.

External Factors: Facing up to US Transregionalism and Multilateral Negotiations

Since the US government lacked the Trade Promotion Authority (TPA)[12] to foster the transregional negotiations in the Americas, the Europeans were not too worried. But in the meantime, the George W. Bush administration — which was determined to complete the FTAA negotiations — obtained the TPA from the Congress. Argentina, which was plunged into an economic crisis lasting four years, mainly as a result of the January 1999 Brazilian currency devaluation, started to have misgivings about the *raison d'être* of Mercosur and wished to become closer to the US in order to foster the FTAA.

Taking into account these different elements as well as the fragility of Mercosur, the US seized the occasion to propose another trade agreement to Argentina. The US hoped to reactivate conflicts among the members of Mercosur and to destabilise the bloc, because from the US viewpoint the FTAA should be made a reality through country–to–country agreements and thus through NAFTA (Santander 2002a, 494–97). By accepting such a proposal, Argentina risked seeing its international negotiating position weakened to the benefit of the US — as had happened when Mexico joined NAFTA (Carranza 2004, 323).

For the EU, a trade agreement between Argentina and the US would represent the end of the South American bloc, threatening the EU's interregionalist strategy towards Mercosur and reinforcing the FTAA project. The EU fears a possible trade–diversion effect from the FTAA on EU economies. For example, when Mexico became a member of NAFTA, European companies lost about half of the Mexican market. The EU wants to avoid this situation happening again with Mercosur (Santander 2002b, 20–28). European leaders are also aware that if the US project became a reality, it would mean an opening of markets and the creation of new standards and rules that would govern international trade. They fear the emergence of a US–led pan–American bloc, which could shape the rules of the worldwide economy (European Economic and Social Committee 2004), thus confirming the theory that interregional and transregional arrangements are also distinguished by their strategic aims (Rüland 2002b, 3–4). Such agreements or projects are often in competition, because they allow a state or regional actors to make up for a lack of international influence or to increase their political presence globally. The strategy of the EU towards South America is a response to the US proposal to create a FTAA. The EU is thus trying to avoid being ousted from that continent. It also wants to avoid losing access to and participation in the development of the new international trade rules.

In order not to be excluded from the shaping of these new rules, Europeans tried to re–launch the interregional process by setting up a 48–million euro package to deepen Mercosur (European Commission 2002, 5). The Union also made a more significant trade proposal during the fifth meeting of the BNC in July 2001, making it clear to South American leaders that if Mercosur breaks down, the EU will not sign a trade agreement with individual countries.

The European proposal included all sectors: fishing, services, industry and agriculture. The EU proposed gradual liberalisation over ten years, covering 100 per cent of manufactured goods and 90 per cent of agricultural produce. By doing so, the EU has again contributed to the survival of Mercosur and encouraged its member countries to come up with a counter–proposal on behalf of their regional bloc. European persistence in recognising and supporting regional groups (Andean Community, Central American Integration System,...) as international actors in their own right has, therefore, contributed to the strengthening of their internal structures and the reinforcement of their negotiation power internationally. That does not mean, of course, that the differences thrown up by the trade negotiations have been erased. In its proposal, the EU did not offer cuts in subsidies; but it did foresee greater liberalisation for products in which Mercosur is interested through the increase in preferential tariff quotas. However, Mercosur member states were disappointed and this was reflected in their proposal. They even proposed a gradual liberalisation over ten years, covering 86 per cent of manufactured goods and 100 per cent of agricultural produce. The car industry, which is a sensitive issue for Mercosur and a priority for the EU, has not been included in the proposal. Moreover, Mercosur countries, and especially Brazil, are very reticent about opening advantages to external competitors in the areas of services, investments and public procurement.

While the proposals of the EU and Mercosur reflect differences of opinion, they formed an important platform for the negotiators from the two regions and allowed them to make progress in the talks. European trade Commissioner Pascal Lamy was determined to conclude an agreement before the end of the Prodi Commission's mandate in 2004 and he was given a date for the finalisation of the negotiations by the EU Council. During the Guadalajara summit between the heads of state and the governments of the EU, Latin America and the Caribbean, the Europeans officially announced an agreement would be concluded in October 2004; according to officials, the chapters on the political dialogue and cooperation were already completed.

This acceleration in the negotiations owes much to the failure of the September 2003 Cancun WTO Ministerial Conference, as well as the race to reach bilateral trade agreements, which were launched by the US to advance the FTAA. After the failure of the WTO Ministerial Conference of Seattle in 1999, the rich countries, and particularly the EU, placed all their hopes in the Cancun meeting. However, the 13 August 2003 compromise reached between Pascal Lamy and his US counterpart, Robert Zoellick, was not to the liking of some 'emerging economic powers' (Brazil, India, South Africa and China) which created the Group of Twenty (G–20). This European–US compromise, which fixed a common position on the opening of the agricultural market, subsidies and antidumping measures, defined in advance the limited scope of any agricultural agreement. In addition, the EU and the US omitted to give detailed figures and a calendar for the reduction of subsidies for the production and exporting of agricultural produce. A second source of contention, which emerged alongside agriculture, were the 'Singapore issues' (investment, competition, transparency of public–procurement markets and trade facilitation) and the liberalisation of services. These issues are of great importance for the transnational companies of rich countries, but problematic for the developing countries. Given that everyone stuck to their line, the split between the rich countries and the G–20 was quickly confirmed, resulting in the failure of the negotiations (Narlikar & Wilkinson 2004).

Faced with this fiasco, the US and the EU embarked on a frantic race to create bilateral agreements. The US has, therefore, demonstrated its will to act by trying to regain control of the negotiation process of the project to integrate the Americas. Eager to make progress with the FTAA, Robert Zoellick signed a Free Trade Agreement with Central America (CAFTA) and has initiated the promotion of bilateral trade agreements with countries such as Columbia, Ecuador, Peru and Bolivia in the belief that they could 'stimulate the FTAA'. Such agreements, which are tailored to suit particular circumstances, are seen by Washington as a means of bolstering its negotiating position and putting the South American bloc, which is in the process of unification, in a difficult situation.[13]

However, the similarities between the participants and between the topics on the WTO agenda and the FTAA agenda make it harder to set up pan–American transregionalism. The FTAA has given rise to reservations within Mercosur, and above all in Brazil, while the US is refusing to do away with protectionism and agricultural subsidies. It is this very same motivation to see agriculture liberalised at a multilateral level that led Brazil and Argentina to ally with approximately twenty countries with different levels of development and differing interests in a whole range of matters on the global trade agenda. In reality, the fate of the FTAA has always depended on WTO agreements, because US negotiators have set themselves the objective of setting up a WTO–plus agreement, according to which concessions made by the countries must exceed those negotiated within the multilateral framework. The failure at Cancun will, therefore, directly affect the FTAA, since, contrary to Washington's wishes, the aspirations for the project will have to be seriously revised and reduced. In a ministerial dispute in Miami on 21 November 2003 between Brazil and the US, which were co–chairing the final phase of negotiations, Brasilia succeeded in convincing others, notably the US authorities, of the need for a small–scale and *à–la–carte* FTAA (dubbed "FTAA–Lite") (Moreira Garcia, 2004, 42). This went against the 'single undertaking' principle made during the ministerial meeting in San José (Costa Rica) in March 1998 and opened up the possibility of creating an international treaty, which included all the topics discussed by the working groups and accepted by all of the parties involved.

In Miami, the FTAA project and Cancun became intertwined. By deciding to negotiate the agricultural dossier solely within the WTO, the Bush administration, therefore, also found itself forced to accept the Brazilian demand to refer negotiations on investment protection, the liberalisation of services, intellectual property and government procurement to the WTO. The Miami compromise allows the thirty–four participating countries to choose the sectors and products in which they would like to participate. Consequently, the project that was still being proposed by the US in the FTAA — and by extension to the south of NAFTA — has been abandoned. To some extent, this is the result of the US turning away from Latin America since the 11 September 2001 attacks, which have focused the country's attention on the fight against terrorism and the wars it has led in Afghanistan and Iraq. Furthermore, the US presidential elections of 2004 prevented the current Bush administration from making any trade concessions, a position that only weakens the US negotiating position under the FTAA project.

As far as the members of the South American bloc are concerned, the Miami agreement is an arrangement that allows Mercosur to focus more calmly on its deepening and enlargement towards the rest of the subcontinent.[14] Moreover, for the Brazilian authorities above all, according to Itamaraty (the Ministry of Foreign Affairs), the Miami Compromise means that the competition mainly from the US and Canada (resulting from a flexible FTAA–Lite) is no longer a threat to the industrial development of Brazil. Mercosur is perceived in Brazil as a means of transforming the country into an industrial power in the region (Turcotte, 2003). It is for this reason that the Brazilian authorities are seeking to establish themselves as the privileged provider of that country's partners for a large number of strategic sectors with high added value, such as capital goods, chemical products, information technology products, motor vehicles and so on.

On behalf of the EU, the European Commission also decided, after the failure of Cancun and within the limits of its mandate, to move forward swiftly on the interregionalist road. Although the FTAA, the trade negotiations between the EU and Mercosur and the WTO constitute three inter–linked processes which are dependent on each other, Mercosur–EU negotiating agenda does not seem to have been affected by the results of the Cancun meeting, unlike the economic integration project of the Americas. The ambitions of the FTAA project have had to be seriously reviewed and reduced. The deadlock in the multilateral talks led the European Commission to forge ahead down the interregional path. The Commission denies that the negotiations with Mercosur are suffering the same fate as those of the FTAA, and continues to advocate a WTO–plus agreement with the South American bloc. It is doing this because such an agreement would allow the EU to forestall the G–20 front, in which Brazil is a leader, and therefore to move ahead more easily in terms of multilateral liberalisation.

To complete the negotiations for an interregional association with Mercosur, in November 2003 the European executive drew up an ambitious working plan known as the 'Brussels Programme', within the limits of its mandate received in June 1999 by the Council of the European Union. This working plan set out five negotiating sessions and two ministerial meetings before October 2004, so as to conclude the Association Agreement with Mercosur before the end of the mandate of the Prodi Commission. The EU trade representative managed to keep the Singapore Issues (investment, competition, transparency of public procurement markets and trade facilitation) which caused so many problems during the meeting in Cancun, on the Mercosur–EU negotiating agenda.

To ensure that the failure of the Cancun negotiations does not jeopardise negotiations between the EU and Mercosur, the European Commission has endeavoured to improve market–access conditions for agricultural products from South America. The innovative aspect of the Commission's proposal lies not in the quota system as such, which was set out in July 2001 at the fifth meeting of the BNC, but rather in the fact that the proposal increases exports from Mercosur countries. In fact, since the Commission has no authority to liberalise these 'sensitive' products, it is drawing up what is known as the 'single pocket principle' to be applied to this quota system. This principle would allow for immediate liberalisation of 50 per cent of export quotas and would make the remaining 50 per cent dependent on the outcome of the Doha round of trade talks. The Commission claims not to be operating two pockets — one for multilateral and one for interregional negotiations — and is trying to ensure that the system avoids making concessions to Mercosur countries twice over.[15]

Moreover, during the third summit between heads of state and government of the EU, Latin America and the Caribbean, held in late May 2004 in Guadalajara, the EU announced officially that an interregional agreement with Mercosur would be signed by 31 October 2004. However that agreement has not been made at the time of writing, due to various difficulties in the trade field. But despite these hindrances to negotiations, the EU is still working towards reaching a WTO–plus agreement during 2005 with Mercosur.

4. Conclusion

Since the early 1990s, various new interregional arrangements have been concluded or are being negotiated. These arrangements can be seen as a corollary of new regionalism, helping to shape the global political economy. New interregionalism as well as new regionalism encourage and legitimise the policies of liberalisation, deregulation and privatisation as part of the development of a globally integrated market. Yet interregionalism also perpetuates trade arrangements with a strong North–South bias. It is often a means to obtain trade concessions when negotiations become blocked at the multilateral level. Hence, this type of relational arrangement is skewed towards economic affairs aimed at opening up markets. The trade negotiations are in conformity with the WTO's rules and disciplines.

Moreover, questions of a political, security, cooperation and/or environmental nature may be addressed in these frameworks. Interregional relations are therefore notable for their strategic nature. The group–to–group strategy of the EU towards Mercosur represents a response to the transregional strategy of the US towards the Americas. Unlike the EU, the US has tried to destabilise Latin American regionalism. The EU constitutes an external federator for regional groups such as Mercosur, which, when facing its European contacts, is under pressure to speak with a single voice. This first involves a considerable effort to harmonise the positions of the South American countries. In addition, the European negotiators are bringing to the negotiating table a number of subjects that are not yet part of common policies within Mercosur. The Southern Cone region's authorities are therefore obliged to develop, with European support, new objectives for their intra–regional agenda. The prospect of concluding an ambitious agreement with the EU increases both the deepening and the international credibility of Mercosur. Although 'new interregionalism' is a result of new regionalism, interregionalism can save and contribute to the consolidation of regional schemes.

Interregionalism is, thus, closely linked to the European Union's intention to play a greater role internationally. The emergence of interregionalist relational arrangements should be seen in the light of this intention. The Union's enthusiasm for negotiating interregional agreements is a "form of economic diplomacy in keeping with the 'gaps' of the CFSP and compensates for the discontinuities of this policy through a broad network of institution-alised cooperation in which not only finance and trade circulate but also 'political principles' and 'values'" (Petiteville 2004, 71). So, in spite of the realists' scepticism about the Union's capacity to play an effective interna-tional role, the EU has succeeded in turning itself into an international actor. The EU has developed external relations that enable it to promote its inter-ests, policies and internal values, while having recourse to cooperative means rather than military might.

Acknowledgements

The author would like to express his gratitude to Fredrik Söderbaum for his very helpful comments. He is also grateful for helpful comments received from Eric Remacle, Mario Telò and Luk van Langenhove. However, the author remains solely responsible for any possible errors or incongruities.

Notes

1. 'European Community' is used here prior to the date of the Maastricht Treaty (1992) which trans-formed the European Community into the European Union.
2. For a detailed analysis of the Rio Process, see Santander (2004a).
3. The political dialogue alludes to the actions and common positions, declarations or diplomatic management. In reality, this dialogue allows the EU to establish diplomatic contacts with third parties. See Gonzalez (1997).
4. For example, services in the areas of education, health (including social services) and culture, as well as questions to do with investment, where the Council makes unanimous decisions.
5. Thanks to Fredrik Söderbaum for elucidating this point to the author.
6. The Andean Pact (currently the Andean Community) was created in 1969. The members are Bolivia, Colombia, Ecuador, Peru and Venezuela. Chile was a founder member but withdrew in 1973, the year Venezuela joined.
7. The Central American Common Market was created in 1960. The members are Costa Rica, El Salvador, Guatemala, Honduras and Nicaragua.
8. Interview European Commission, DG Enterprise (26 April 2004).
9. According to the theory, membership of transregional arrangements "is more diffuse than in traditional group–to–group dialogues; it does not necessarily coincide with regional groupings and may include member states from more than two regions", while hybrid agreements constitute a relationship between regional groupings and single powers. Hänggi, (2000), pp. 6–7.
10. COPA: Committee of Agricultural Organisations in the European Union; COGECA: General Confederation of Agricultural Cooperatives in the European Union.
11. This idea encompasses the view that agricultural production also takes account of food security, landscape conservation, the protection of animals and employment, etc. Laurent (2001).
12. Authority given to the executive power by the legislative power to negotiate trade deals and submit them for approval without possibility for amendments.
13. One should not forget that Brazil, supported by the others members of Mercosur, played a crucial role in the creation of the G–20, which managed to block negotiations in Cancun, to the great displeasure of the US and the EU.
14. A new step has been accomplished in favour of the South America integration. Indeed, Mercosur, CAN, Chile, Guyana and Surinam signed an agreement, in December 2004 in Cusco (Peru), establishing the South American Community of Nations. Bilbao (2004).
15. Interview with the European Commission, DG Agriculture, 27 April 2004.

References

Bergsten, F. C. (1996) Globalizing Free Trade: The Ascent of Regionalism, *Foreign Affairs* 3, May/June, pp. 105–120.

Bilbao, L. (2004) Comunidad Sudamericana de Naciones, *el Dipló*, December, Available at: http://www.eldiplo.org/semanales.php3, accessed January 2005).

Cammack, P. (1999) Mercosur: From Domestic Concerns to Regional Influence, in: G. Hook & I. Kearns (eds), *Subregionalism and World Order*, pp. 95–115 (Great Britain: Macmillan Press Ltd).

Carranza, M. E. (2004) Mercosur and the End Game of the FTAA Negotiations: Challenges and Prospects after the Argentine Crisis, *Third World Quarterly*, 25(2), pp. 319–337.

Cienfuegos M. M. (2003) Implications of European Union Enlargement for Euro–Mercosur Relations, in: E. Barbé & E. Johansson–Nogués (eds) *Beyond Enlargement: The New Members and New Frontiers of the Enlarged European Union*, pp. 257–289 (Barcelona: IUEE).

COPA (2004) EU–Mercosur negotiations represent a big risk for European agriculture, CdP(04)13–1, 27 April.

de Wilde d'Estmael, T. (1998) *La dimension politique des relations économiques extérieures de la Communauté européenne* (Bruxelles: Bruylant).

ECLAC (2000) Spain Foreign Investment and Corporate Strategies in Latin America and the Caribbean, in: ECLAC (ed.) *Foreign Investment in Latin America and the Caribbean 1999*, (Chile: ECLAC).

European Commission (1994a) Documento básico sobre las relaciones de la Unión Europea con América Latina y Caribe, Organisation des Etats Ibero–américains. 31 October. Electronic version: www.campus–oei.org/oeivirt/rie07a08.htm, accessed August 2004).

European Commission (1994b) Hacia un fortalecimiento de la política de la Unión Europea respecto al Mercosur. COM (94) 428 final, 19 October.

European Commission (1995a) Appui de la Communauté européenne aux efforts d'intégration économique régionale des pays en développement. COM (95) 219 final.

European Commission (1995b) Unión Europea y América Latina: Actualidad y perspectivas del fortalecimiento de la asociación, 1996–2000. COM(95) 495 final.

European Commission (1995c) Free Trade Areas: An appraisal. SEC(95) 322 final.

European Commission (2002) Mercosur–European Union Regional Strategy Paper 2002–2006. CSP Mercosur 10.09.2002.

European Commission's Enterprise Desk (2004a) Mercosur–EU Business Forum (MEBF). 3 June. Available at: http://europa.eu.int/comm/enterprise/enterprise_policy/business_dialogues/mebf/mebfoverview.htm, accessed August 2004).

European Commission's Enterprise Desk (2004b) Business roundtables and dialogues. Overview. 3 June. Available at: http://europa.eu.int/comm/enterprise/enterprise_policy/business_dialogues/index.htm, accessed August 2004).

European Commission Mercosur Desk (2000) Basic information on Mercosur. June.

European Council (1994) Conclusions de la présidence, Essen. SI (94) 1000, 10 December.

European Economic and Social Committee (1996) Avis du 25 octobre 1995 sur la communication de la Commission au Conseil et Parlement européen pour un renforcement de la politique de l'UE à l'égard du Mercosur. Official Journal C, 22 January.

European Economic and Social Committee (2004) Repercussions of the Free Trade Area of the Americas Agreement on EU relations with Latin America and the Caribbean, Opinion of the EESC. REX/135 — EESC 314/2004 id.

European Parliament (1995) Rapport sur la communication de la Commission au Conseil et au Parlement européen pour un renforcement de la politique de l'Union européenne à l'égard du Mercosur, Working Document. 12 April.

European Parliament (1999) Declaración de Río de Janeiro, América Latina/Caribe/Unión Europea: Primera Cumbre. Press Release, 29 June, Brussels. Available at: www.europarl.eu.int/delegations/noneurope/idel/d12/docs/cumbrederio/declaracionfinales.htm, accessed [date]).

European Union, *Selected instruments taken from Treaties*. Electronic version: http://europa.eu.int/abc/obj/treaties/fr/frtr2b.htm, accessed August 2004).

Gamble, A. & Payne A. (1996) *Regionalism and World Order* (London: Macmillan Press Ltd).

Gill, S. (1995) *American Hegemony and the Trilateral Commission* (New York: Cambridge University Press).

Giordano, P. & Santiso, J. (2000) La course aux Amériques: les stratégies des investisseurs Européens dans le Mercosur, *Problèmes d'Amérique latine* 39, October/December, pp. 55–87.

Gonzalez Sanchez, E. (1997) El dialogo político de la Unión Europea con países terceros, *Revista de derecho comunitario europeo* 1, January/June, pp. 69–94.

Grugel, J. (2002) Spain, the European Union and Latin America: Governance and Identity in the Making of 'New' Interregionalism, paper presented at the conference 'The Spanish Presidency of the European Union', University of Liverpool, 12 October.

Hänggi, H. (2000) Interregionalism: Empirical and Theoretical Perspectives, paper presented at the workshop 'Dollars, Democracy and Trade: External Influence on Economic Integration in the Americas', Los Angeles, 18 May.

Hettne, B. (2001) Europeanization of Europe: the longer view, paper presented at the '4th Pan-European Conference of International Relations', Canterbury, 8–10 September.

Higgott, R. (1997) Mondialisation et gouvernement : l'émergence du niveau régional, *Politique étrangère* 2, pp. 277–292.

Hill, C. (1993) The capability–expectations gap, or conceptualizing Europe's international role, *Journal of Common Market Studies* 31(3), pp. 305–328.

Hillcoat, G. (1997) Les relations extérieures du Mercosur: bilan et perspectives, *Problèmes d'Amérique latine* 26 July/September, pp. 101–125.

IRELA (1999a) Las perspectivas de un acuerdo de libre comercio UE–Mercosur y las opciones para la política de EE UU (Madrid: IRELA).

IRELA (1999b) Relaciones Económicas entre el Mercosur y la UE: perpectivas para la nueva década (Madrid: IRELA).

Laurent, C. (2001) La multifoncionnalité de l'agriculture, in: P. Giordano, A. Valladaõ and M.-F. Durand (ed.) *Vers un accord entre l'Europe et le Mercosur*, pp. 407–423 (Paris: Presses de Sciences Po).

Marchand, M. H., Boas, M. & Shaw T. (1999) The Political Economy of New Regionalisms, *Third World Quarterly* 20(5), pp. 897–910.

Mearsheimer, J. J. (1990) Back to the Future: Instability in Europe after the Cold War, *International Security* 15(2), pp. 194–199.

Moreira Garcia, C. (2004) Negociaciones comerciales OMC–ALCA : Será 2004 una buena cosecha ?, *Política Exterior* 97, pp. 39–43.

Narlikar, A. & Wilkinson, R. (2004) Collapse at the WTO: a Cancun post-mortem, *Third World Quarterly* 25(3), pp. 447–460.

Official Journal of the Communities (1994) Déclaration commune solennelle entre le Conseil de l'UE et la Commission européenne, d'une part, et les Etats membres du Mercosur, d'autre part, C 377 31 December.

Payne, A. (1996) The United States and its Enterprise for the Americas, in: A. Gamble & A. Payne (ed.) *Regionalism and World Order*, pp. 93–129 (London: Macmillan).

Petiteville, F. (1997) Les processus d'intégration régionale, vecteurs de structurations du système international ? *Etudes Internationales* XXVIII, pp. 511–533.

Petiteville, F. (2002) L'Union européenne, acteur international «global»? Un agenda de recherche, *La revue internationale et stratégique* 47, pp. 145–157.

Petiteville, F. (2004) L'Union dans les relations internationales: du soft power à la puissance?, *Questions internationales* 7, May/June, pp. 63–72.

Regelsberger, E. (1998) Group-to-Group Dialogues — a Prominent Role in the EU's External Relations, *CFSP Forum*, pp. 2–3.

Remacle, E. (2000) De l'Euro à la PESC, d'Amsterdam à Helsinki: les balbutiements d'un «acteur» international, *Annuaire français de relations internationales* I, pp. 487–501.

Rubio, L. A. (2004) L'intégration centre–américaine : entre le modèle européen et le modèle nord–américain, in: S. Santander (ed.) *Globalisation, gouvernance et logiques régionales dans les Amériques*, pp. 119–142 (Brussels/Paris: L'Harmattan/GELA–IS).

Rüland, J. (2002a) Inter- and Transregionalism: Remarks on the State of the Art of a New Research Agenda, *National Europe Centre Paper* n° 35, University of Freiburg.

Rüland, J. (2002b) Interregionalism in International Relations, *Working Paper* 11, April, University of Freiburg.

Santander, S. (2000a) Aux origines de la globalisation, in F. Nahavandi *Globalisation et néolibéralisme dans le tiers–monde*, pp. 29–42 (Paris: L'Harmattan).

Santander, S. (2000b), Globalisation et néorégionalisme: déclin ou redéfinition du rôle de l'Etat sur la scène internationale?, *Studia Diplomatica* LIII(5), pp. 93–108.

Santander, S. (2001) La légitimation de l'Union européenne par l'exportation de son modèle d'intégration et de gouvernance régionale. Le cas du Marché Commun du Sud, *Etudes internationales* XXXIII(1), pp. 51–67.

Santander, S. (2002a) EU–Mercosur interregionalism: Facing up to the South American crisis and the emerging Free Trade Area of the Americas, *European Foreign Affairs Review* 7(4), pp. 491–505.

Santander, S. (2002b) Reactivación de las negociaciones Euro–MERCOSUR bajo el temor del "síndrome mejicano"?, *Revista de Derecho International y del Mercosur*, 6(1), pp. 20–28.

Santander, S. (2004a) La stratégie latino–américaine de l'Union européenne: vers un étiolement du processus de Rio?, in: P. Magnette (ed.) *La grande Europe*, pp. 369–388 (Brussels: Editions de l'Université de Bruxelles).

Santander, S. (2004b) Globalisation, logiques régionales et gouvernance dans les Amériques, in : S. Santander (ed.) *Globalisation, gouvernance et logiques régionales dans les Amériques*, pp. 5–42 (Brussels/Paris: L'Harmattan/GELA–IS).

Sautter, C. (1996) La découverte des pays émergents, *Commentaire* 76, pp. 871–878.

Smith, M. & Woolcock, S. (1999) European Commercial Policy: a Leadership Role in the New Millennium, *European Foreign Affairs Review*, 4(4), pp. 439–62.

Stopford, J. M. & Strange, S. (1991) *Rival States, Rival Firms: Competition for World Market Shares* (Cambridge: Cambridge University Press).

Telò, M. (1998) L'Union européenne dans le monde de l'après–guerre froide, in: M. Telò & P. Magnette (eds) *De Maastricht à Amsterdam*, pp. 23–65 (Brussels: Complexe).

Telò, M. (2001) *European Union and New Regionalism: Regional Actors and Global Governance in a Post-hegemonic Era* (England: Ashgate).

Ténier, J. (2003) *Intégrations régionales et mondialisation* (Paris: La documentation française).

Turcotte, S. F. (2003) Le multilatéralisme brésilien et le libre–échange dans les Amériques, in: C. Deblock and S. F. Turcotte, *Suivre les Etats–Unis ou prendre une autre voie?* pp. 81–110 (Brussels: Bruylant).

Waltz, K. (1993) The New World Order, *Millennium* 22, pp. 187–195.

New Interregionalism? The EU and East Asia

JULIE GILSON

1. Introduction

> "Given the sprawling variety of Asia, it is absurd to think of a monolithic EU–Asia relationship". (Patten 2002)

This statement by former EU External Relations Commissioner Christopher Patten illustrates the complexities facing the EU when its member states seek to formulate and sustain relations with the countries of Asia. Indeed, the European Commission divides its relations with the broader region into South Asia, Northeast Asia, Southeast Asia, Central Asia, Australasia and bilateral (state–to–state) relationships. How, then, is it possible to talk of a 'region–to–region dialogue', or the concept of interregionalism, with reference to this "sprawling variety"? This article examines how the EU utilizes interregionalism as one mechanism for managing economic and political relations with a growing yet disparate region and how, in so doing, it may influence and shape the very concept of an East Asian region. The development of the ASEAN (Association of Southeast Asian Nations) Plus Three (APT) process and growing intra–regional dynamics have been reinforced by participation in explicitly interregional formats (namely EU–ASEAN dialogue and the Asia–Europe Meeting, ASEM), with the effect that EU representatives often single out the East Asian dimension, comprising Southeast and North-east Asia.[1]

The fifth Asia–Europe Meeting (ASEM) took place in Hanoi in September 2004 under the umbrella theme of 'Further Revitalising and Substantiating the Asia–Europe Partnership'. The twenty–five original member states had grown to thirty–nine, with the inclusion of the newest members of ASEAN and the ten new members of the EU, following their accession in May 2004. Reflecting upon the eight–year history of the interregional encounter, leaders noted in particular that economic cooperation, fortified by the 'Hanoi Declaration on Closer Economic Partnership' should be complemented by the political initiatives enshrined in their 'Declaration on Multilateralism': "ASEM Ministers reaffirmed their commitment to multilateralism and to a fair and just rules–based international order, with a strong United Nations at its heart, to resolve international disputes, to promote positive aspects of globalization, and to advance democratization of international relations" (MOFA 2004).

Based on the four principles of informality, multi–dimensionality, equal partnership and a high–level focus, ASEM presents the EU with a useful mechanism for managing relations with thirteen different economies, promoting democratic values and the pursuit of human rights among states whose record has yet to satisfy European demands, and balancing geostrategic interests in a volatile and rapidly changing region. It serves not only as an overarching framework in which to express a range of themes that are pursued simultaneously in bilateral agreements, but also as the very locus for such bilateral encounters. In these ways, and as this analysis will demonstrate, ASEM delineates a generic context for interaction.

For the participating states of East Asia, the ASEM process offers a means of dealing collectively with twenty–five states, provides a first–hand examination of the practices of regional integration and establishes a framework in which East Asia can present itself as a regional political and economic entity and realize the 'third side' in a global triangle of regional economic blocs (Pou Serradell 1996, 191; CAEC 1996; Maull *et al.* 1998, xiv). In these ways, then, ASEM is one of a number of foreign policy tools available to the EU and serves several important functions. Nevertheless, it is not intended as a replacement for other forms of engagement. Indeed, as will be shown, it may represent an historical moment in the building up of a variety of relations.

The first section of this analysis considers the relevance of interregionalism for this case study. The second section examines the driving forces in the EU behind policies towards East Asia, and part three assesses the development of a regional identity within East Asia itself in response to this region–to–region process. It also examines the growing role of non–state actors within the ASEM process. The final section locates the type of region–to–region arrangement between Europe and East Asia in relation to other kinds of interregional frameworks available to the EU.

2. Defining Interregionalism

Interregionalism

Interregionalism represents the interaction of one region with another. Although ASEM is not a gathering of two pre–existing regions, the decision to enshrine the concept of equal partnership within it represented an explicit attempt by member states not to follow a transregionalist path, such as the APEC model, but to create a region–to–region dialogue. Interregionalism is often portrayed as a 'double regional project', responding to the need to pool an ever greater percentage of resources in recognition of other interregional or global dynamics. Alternatively, it is understood as a process of regional emulation, in which existing regions trigger the formation of new ones, with potentially positive or negative consequences (Hettne *et al.* 1999, xxii). In these ways, the rise of interregionalism is often witnessed as a means of managing relations in a globalising world.

Interregionalism also has implications for the very nature of the regions involved. The functional requirements of the ASEM arrangement mean that, while the European Commission and Council represent the EU in ASEM, the East Asian contingent, too, has to make intra–regional agreements prior to meetings with its European partner and is also represented by two Asian coordinating countries in rotation. East Asian participants meet in their collective capacity as 'Asia', in order to frame a collective response prior to Asia–Europe meetings. Thus, the region as a political actor is central to interregionalism, in a way that is not the case in transregional arrangements (Aggarwal & Fogarty 2004). At the same time, however, the East Asian contingent has, to a large extent, to invent an 'Asianness' upon which to build its regional position in the face of a definite counterpart (the EU) and this leaves open the question of what type of region is likely to emerge. In these ways, beyond narrow interpretations of regional integration, ASEM does indeed create a 'regional' space around which the states of East Asia may coalesce in a number of spheres.

'Self' and 'Other'

One way to comprehend the distinctiveness of a region–to–region framework is to focus on the way it posits a given 'self' interacting with a specific 'other'. Drawing on the work of John Searle, self/other relations may be understood in two principal ways (Searle 1995). First, the self may be formed and reformed in the very process of looking at an other and reflecting back on the self. In this way, the self may be identified through a process of "differentiation" with an other, drawing on its distinct identity. Second, the self may be understood as being formed from the start by the very act of being in a relationship with an other. In this way, the identity of the self is intrinsically linked with the process of "engaging" with that other (Campbell 1998, 9 & 70–3). Put simply, interregionalism may not only represent the conjoining of two independent regions, but may be regarded as a process whereby, through their mutual interaction, the regions of East Asia and Europe come to recognize themselves as such (Scholte 1996, 70). One only has to visit the EU website and examine the trade figures for 'ASEM Asia' to see how this form of Asia has already gained currency as a way of summarising the collection of East Asian states. Interregionalism, then, provides a locus within which a "public reality" enables regions to talk to one another as regional actors (Searle 1995, 127 & 190). As practices of interaction continue, ideas and understandings of self and other are constantly formed and reformed, to the extent that, without the other, the self would be incomprehensible, since that other "clothes us in comprehensibility" (Sampson 1993, 106).

Given the nature of the regions in ASEM (or indeed the EU–ASEAN dialogue), to what extent does this form of interregionalism contribute to the development of a notion of region within East Asia? (Searle 1995, 127) A region may, in fact, derive its own identity in part as a result of being accepted as a 'region' by a discernible and pre–defined regional other and existing through the process of reciprocal achievements.[2] Does the form of 'implicit we–ness' found in groups such as the East Asian contingent of ASEM offer a sense of identity born from the very need to *act* as a region in responding to other perceived regions? Moreover, can the collective 'we' in the case of ASEM in turn become the dominant 'we' for all aspects of external ('East Asian') interaction? (Wendt 1994, 386). Interregionalism may not 'create' the region in the case of ASEM, but it may act as an "intra–regional mobilizing agent", both in advancing the EU's external regional profile and in advancing the development of an East Asian regional consciousness (Higgott 1994, 368). In summary, interregionalism may work in both functional and cognitive ways: as a tool for managing disparate relations, and as a means potentially of (re–) defining concepts of region. The following section examines how interregionalism in the form of ASEM may be viewed as the conjuncture of different interregional and intra–regional histories.

3. Developing Interregional Encounters

EU–ASEAN Relations

For centuries different parts of Asia have attracted European missionary, trading and colonial interests (Gilson 2002, 31; Lach 1965). From the extensive regional interests of the British and Dutch East India Companies, as well as the claims of their governments, to French colonial ambitions in

Indochina, much of the region was covered by European footsteps (Colbert 1992; Dixon 1991, 121). Indeed, European imprints on the region can still be seen in the very names accorded to different areas, such as Mountbatten's definition of "Southeast Asia" itself (SarDesai 1997, 3). In the aftermath of the Second World War, many states of Southeast Asia were engaged in a fight for national independence and the difficulties and challenges such freedoms brought with them, while Japan, for its part, was forced to come to terms with defeat and the need to rebuild a shattered economy (Hook *et al.* 2001). There was scant opportunity for regional developments in those first postwar decades and no attempt to emulate the European Coal and Steel Community of the 1950s. The Federation of Malaysia was created in 1963, but lasted in that form only until 1965 when Singapore was expelled (SarDesai 1997, 288). The Southeast Asian Treaty Organisation (SEATO) was set up in 1954, but primarily as a means of promoting US military aims within the region and locking Southeast Asia into the 'western' camp in the rapidly escalating Cold War. Although the 1967 establishment of ASEAN was considered as a further step towards strengthening anti–communist support within Asia, it was also viewed by its founding members to offer a mechanism for the resolution of intra–regional disputes, particularly over territorial claims.[3] In 1976, as a result of concerns over the potential power of Vietnam and fears of communist uprisings across the region, ASEAN's Bali Summit enshrined the Declaration of ASEAN Concord and Treaty of Amity and Concord and laid the foundations for cooperation in international organisations and even with regard to military issues (Colbert 1992, 250–251). Prior to entering into a region–to–region engagement with the EU, therefore, Southeast Asia had fully established an intra–regional existence through which to negotiate collectively with regard to a range of issues. This network would also underpin attempts, advocated by the likes of Malaysian Prime Minister Mahathir bin Mohamed, to pursue a 'Look East' policy in favour of closer Asian cooperation; it would further champion 'Asian values'; and it would provide the functional basis for further institutional endeavours, including the ASEAN Regional Forum (ARF) and ASEM (Chan 1998; See also Europa 2004a). The leaders of ASEAN further strengthened their own grouping during their Bali Summit in October 2003, when they lay down plans for the creation of an ASEAN Economic, Security and Socio–Cultural Community.

Against this background of regional developments within East Asia, the EU (then EC) began biennial foreign ministers meetings with ASEAN in 1978 and signed a Cooperation Agreement with the Association in 1980. Supervised by the EC–ASEAN Joint Co–operation Committee (JCC), the EU–ASEAN relationship today is pursued through region–to–region ministerial meetings, as part of the EU–ASEAN dialogue, and through individual EC–ASEAN Cooperation Agreements (to which Myanmar is not a signatory). In 2002, the EU was ASEAN's second largest export market and the third largest trading partner after the US and Japan, while the 'New Partnership with Southeast Asia' of July 2003 codified an ongoing EU commitment to the region.

EU–SAARC Relations

In many ways, during the late 1970s and 1980s, the EU's relations with the South Asia Association for Regional Cooperation (SAARC) initially followed the same pattern.[4] SAARC was established in 1985 and, given the difficulties between its two main member states (India and Pakistan), has focused on technical issues and the pursuit of an eventual South Asian Economic Union, for which the EU has always provided the model. In January 2004 its leaders signed a South Asia Free Trade Area, to come into force in January 2006. Having established cooperation agreements with the individual states of the Association during the 1970s, the EC/EU signed a memorandum of understanding with SAARC in July 1986. In order to avoid contentious political issues, it was based on technical issues only and was designed to promote economic and social development in South Asia, using EU expertise, advice and training.[5] At the initiative of Sri Lanka, the first dialogue took place in 1998 and, since that time, the two sides have discussed regional issues related to health, the environment and the trafficking of people and drugs and, in 1999, proposed a mission to create an assistance programme to aid the integration processes in South Asia. One further important measure pertains to the implementation of the GSP (Generalised System of Preferences) Cumulative Clause of the Rules of Origin. The GSP itself was designed to facilitate economic development by offering preferential tariffs to developing countries. In practice, the cumulative clause means that the EU will provide GSP facilities to products from any SAARC country and demonstrates the ongoing donor–recipient arrangement among the two regions. This is in contradistinction to the assumption that Southeast Asia, no longer as dependent on the GSP scheme, has 'graduated' to become a trading partner with the EU, a status that is reinforced by the stated 'equal partnership' of the ASEM and EU–ASEAN arrangements.

The region–to–region dialogue has also been used to enhance bilateral relations and, for example, an EU–India dialogue was begun in 2000, primarily as a channel for promoting trade and investment. At their fifth summit in the Hague in November 2004, Indian Prime Minister Manmohan Singh and Commission President Romano Prodi set down their plans for the development of, *inter alia*, an Action Plan, a dialogue on disarmament and non–proliferation, an exchange among parliamentarians and the creation of an Energy Panel. Today, the EU is the largest trading partner of India, Pakistan and Bangladesh and an important trading partner for Sri Lanka, Maldives, Bangladesh and Nepal (Kumar 2004). Relations with this region continue to expand, but with a different focus from the explicitly interregional dialogue with East Asia.

Expanding Interregional Relations

Given the central regional role played by ASEAN, it is no surprise that the 1995 proposal for ASEM came from the then Prime Minister of Singapore Goh Chok Tong (Camroux & Lechervy 1996). Advocating closer linkages with the growing EU, as well as encouraging the participation of their dominant neighbours, China, Japan and South Korea, ASEM was seen not only to offer closer links with the expanding EU, but also to provide the Southeast Asian community with a chance to garner greater leverage in the face of the forces of globalisation, to balance the potential rivalry between Japan and China, and to moderate the effects of any future change in the US geostrategic position in the region. For the EU it offered a welcome opportunity to embrace a region of dynamic growth, which had been largely neglected by European businesses. The extension of EU–ASEAN relations to include the states of China, Japan and South Korea also served another purpose for the EU. Having made agreements with Laos and Cambodia in July 2000, the EU was unable to extend this to Burma/Myanmar, due to Myanmar's democratic and human rights record which the EU viewed as unsatisfactory. EU–ASEAN relations effectively reached an *impasse* over this issue, as the EU refused to participate in any initiatives involving ASEAN's acceding member state. However, the ASEM process effectively re–ignited their relations and the April 2000 EU General Affairs Council approved an arrangement for the Burmese Foreign Minister to participate in EU–ASEAN ministerial meetings, while at the same time announcing a toughening of the EU Common Position on Myanmar. The wider scope of membership and issues covered by ASEM offered a means of subsuming this bilateral problem within a broader framework and, although this issue continues to simmer, it does not threaten the dialogue itself.

The idea that ASEM strengthens the East Asia–Europe side of the three "fundamental poles of the international order" has become a well–used rationale for East Asia–Europe developments (Pou Serradell 1996, 191; CAEC 1996; Maull *et al.* 1998, xiv). Thus, the 'tripolarisation' of the global economy becomes the mantra of ASEM's advancement, with the resulting reasoning that if ASEM did not exist it would have to be invented (Dent 1999, 390). Leaders at that first summit discussed a range of economic, political and cultural issues, and issued statements making explicit reference to the interregionalism represented by the summit itself.[6] Not only did this opportunity represent a growth in "confidence and reciprocal understanding 'between two of the' most important regions of the world",[7] but developments since 1996 have also "emphasised the mutual inter–dependence of [the] two regions, and the value of the ASEM process in enhancing Asia–Europe dialogue and cooperation" (European Commission 2000).

Early initiatives were driven in the main by Southeast Asian nations. It was, nevertheless, clear from the start that Japan, China and South Korea would constitute an integral part of the East Asian contingent, since their participation would distinguish the arrangement from those (especially EU–ASEAN dialogue) already in place. This new forum offered ASEAN the opportunity to play a central role in a new international framework: Thailand hosted the first summit, Singapore houses the Asia–Europe Foundation (ASEF), and Malaysia was the recipient of the first major regional project. ASEM also enabled Southeast Asian participants to cooperate alongside

China, whose participation was seen to be crucial for regional and interregional economic relations and security. Finally, ASEM facilitated a shared interest by Europeans and Asians in retaining a predicable and stable US presence in the region (Shin & Segal 1997).

Interregional Summitry

Biennial summits represent the apex of a host of activities held in the name of ASEM and are useful in charting the type of dialogue between the two partners. The first summit was held in Bangkok in February 1996, with the aim of launching the whole ASEM process and facilitating dialogue among the leaders of the participating countries. Subjects covered during the first summit included activities in the field of trade, science and technology, environmental cooperation, anti–terrorist measures and the combating of the illegal trafficking of drugs. ASEM's very existence was regarded by several observers as a significant step forward in the promotion of East Asia–Europe relations.[8] Cooperation in this form, then, may be viewed as a means of achieving relative gains, or as a learning channel for joint problem–solving (Gamble & Payne 1996, 5).

The second ASEM summit took place in London in April 1998. The prepared agenda had to be modified as a consequence of the 1997 Asian currency crises and discussion in London became mired in the details of how to remedy the problems presented by them. Hence, on this second occasion it was not the potential success so much as the potential failure of East Asia that dominated leaders' concerns. Although the second summit achieved only limited tangible results (such as the Investment Promotion Action Plan and the ASEM Trust Fund), a certain idea of these two regions seemed to have become embedded within the ASEM framework. In some ways, too, the 'Asian' crisis reinforced the notion — particularly from outside the region — that an East Asia region did exist.[9] The second summit also challenged the notion of neutrality, which should facilitate the discussion of potentially contentious issues, such as the need for good governance and human rights. The report of the so–called 'Vision Group' of 'wise men' set up after ASEM 2 demonstrates how much more ASEM could actually do, and focused, amongst other issues, on the lack of attention paid to human rights and different opinions regarding the opening of markets within the ASEM process. NGOs commenting on ASEM have also noted that human rights cannot be ignored in the pursuit of improved international relations. In this area in particular, given the learning capacity of the ASEM framework, there is a clear opportunity to strengthen the links between human rights and personal freedoms and the pursuit of economic development and political equality. Although ASEM has provided a convenient mechanism by which to address, in part, the ongoing problem of Myanmar within the EU–ASEAN dialogue, to date the opportunity for an expanded dialogue regarding human rights has not been embraced.

ASEM 3, held in Seoul in October 2000, was also overtaken by events, although this time of a more positive nature. It followed the historic June

2000 summit between South Korean President Kim Dae–Jung and his North Korean counterpart, Kim Jong–Il, which re–ignited hopes of reconciliation. What is more, shortly before the interregional summit Kim Dae Jung had also received the Nobel Prize for Peace. As a result, ASEM 3 was able to produce a separate statement on the developments on the Korean peninsula, known as the 'Seoul Declaration for Peace on the Korean Peninsula'.[10] Other topics under discussion included the particular issues of East Timor and Kosovo, as well as perennial concerns over UN reform, arms control and calls for the completion of signatures to the Comprehensive Test Ban Treaty (CTBT). In this way and over a wide range of subjects, ASEM was viewed by one observer as opening new "channels through which bargaining takes place and leverage can be exerted" (Smith 1998, 312).

ASEM 4, in Copenhagen in September 2002, was a somewhat muted affair, with a focus on historical civilizations as its centrepiece, through a retreat entitled 'Dialogue on Cultures and Civilizations'. It did provide an opportunity to discuss international agenda, including anti–terrorism, for which a separate Declaration on Cooperation against International Terrorism was issued, but this declaration replicated the general statements by government representatives that had been made in the wake of the 11 September 2001 attacks in New York.

The fifth summit in Hanoi in September 2004 continued these discussions and raised important issues about the nature of this interregional gathering. To begin with, the newly acceded ten member states of the EU were represented at ASEM 5. In addition, the most recent three new states of ASEAN, including Myanmar, were also able to join. As a result, the meeting not only drew attention to what it regarded as the positive effects of EU expansion, but also to the trends towards closer cooperation in East Asia, particularly the plans for an ASEAN Community by 2020 and enhanced collaboration through the APT process.

Non–State Actors

The growth of activities under the three–pillared framework of ASEM has also facilitated the greater inclusion of non–state representatives. In the context of ASEM, two groups are important, namely, business communities and non–governmental organisations (NGOs). Business interests lie at the heart of ASEM's first pillar of trade issues and are included as part of official discussions, notably through the Asia–Europe Business Forum (AEBF). This inclusion was intended to enhance region–to–region business dialogue and led to the establishment of a number of working groups and *ad hoc* meetings, whose conclusions are discussed with and by the 'senior officials meeting on trade and investment' (SOMTI), as well as foreign and economic ministers meetings.

The first AEBF was held in Paris in October 1996, where it set out aims to promote business–to–business and business–government dialogue, within a non–discriminatory framework and alongside specific recommendations relating to infrastructure, small and medium–sized enterprises (SMEs), financial services, the Europe–Asia Infrastructure Fund and the promotion of SME partnerships (Gilson 2002, 75–8). Different working groups were tasked to examine particular aspects of trade relations, such as intellectual property rights (IPR) or investment. A particular focus on SMEs led to attempts to facilitate the exchange of information and expertise and to the creation of the Trade Facilitation Action Plan (TFAP) and the Investment Promotion Action Plan (IPAP). The success of these endeavours to date is hard to measure, particularly as SMEs do not represent an homogeneous group of business interests and concerns. Nevertheless, the ninth Asia–Europe Business Forum, held in Hanoi just prior to the fifth ASEM summit in 2004, agreed to set up a core Business Advisory Council to make recommendations to ASEM, thereby suggesting that ASEM's broad form of interregionalism offers a complementary space for the advancement of business initiatives (see Vietnam Gateway 2005).

The role of NGOs with regard to ASEM has been somewhat different from that of businesses, since this sector has never been welcomed into the official track of interregional dialogue. In fact, the ASEM process, here too, opens up a space for participation, as articulated in the chair's statement at ASEM 3, which outlines the role of the third pillar of 'Promoting Cooperation in Other Areas, including Social and Cultural Issues':

> Leaders underscored the importance of enhancing mutual understanding between the two regions through closer people–to–people exchanges of various kinds in the social and cultural areas. Leaders also recognized the vivid and diverse cultures of Asia and Europe as a source of vitality to enliven the mutual cooperation between the two regions and noted that ASEM is an excellent vehicle to achieve this end.[11]

People–to–people exchanges, however, were not designed to include NGO activities, especially as many of the participating member states in East Asia do not have a tradition of free and critical NGO groups (Schmit 1996, 178–187). Rather, ASEF was tasked with developing exchanges among groups such as students, academics, journalists and 'young leaders'.[12] A number of calls have been made, notably from the European Parliament, for inclusion within the ASEM process of NGOs, but to date their presence has been tolerated only on the sidelines.[13]

In response to the planned exclusion of civil society interests, a Europe–Asia Forum in Venice in January 1996 between 'civil societies' resulted in the establishment of the first Joint Asia–Europe NGO Conference alongside the first ASEM summit. Since then, ASEM summits have provided a frame of reference for the development of peripheral Asia–Europe People's Forums (AEPF), representing a coalition of multiple interests. The AEPF participated alongside ASEM2, 3 and 4 with growing recognition. In addition, lobby tours of Europe and Asia were arranged for May 2000, to highlight the concerns of civil society *vis–à–vis* ASEM, to stimulate public debate on ASEM in parliaments and the media, and to profile the issues articulated within the 'People's

Agenda'. The fifth AEPF took place in Hanoi on the margins of ASEM 5. Its aims were to address the two major themes of the social dimensions of trade and investment and global security, including human security.

The actions of NGO groups to date as part of the broader ASEM process demonstrate that, particularly in the face of new and global threats, region–to–region networks of communication and exchange may link local, regional and international political agendas (Princen 1994, 333). Indeed, at this level, such NGO coalitions "are not about influencing structures, so much as creating them" (Finger 1994, 59). Rather, their participation, like those of the business community and the growing profile of regions themselves, need to be viewed as part of a changing international context. Thus, although the 'Battle for Seattle' paradigm has tended to portray the role of civil society as an organic rebellion against the imposition of globalising forces, broad attention to NGOs from Rio in 1992 to Jubilee 2000 sets the context for NGO participation on the sidelines of ASEM (Scholte 2000, 116). As a result, NGOs within the ASEM process have slowly gained "negotiated access" or "controlled inclusion", through the spaces created by its interregional structures (Richards 2000, 9).

This section has illustrated the disparate forces that coalesced in the formation of ASEM. The following section examines the particular motivations within Europe and East Asia for participation in this interregional context.

4. EU Driving Forces for Relations with East Asia

Asia: Strategy Paper

A number of important documents have advanced the EU's generic policy towards Asia. The first one was the 1994 'Towards a New Asia Strategy', which raised a number of key issues of joint interest, such as sustainable development, the protection of the environment, the development of the information society, forest preservation and AIDS research, as well as cooperation towards global economic stability, China's full participation in the World Trade Organisation and open and equitable competition.[14] This paper was updated in September 2001 with the publication of the European Commission's Communication, entitled "Europe and Asia: A Strategic Framework for Enhanced Partnership". This communication further clarified the intra–regional changes within the EU and Asia, against the background of which EU–Asia dialogue could take place. Its main aims were to promote peace and security in Asia, enhance mutual trade and investment, pursue poverty alleviation, promote human rights and democracy, develop further global partnerships, and encourage an increased awareness of the EU in Asia, and *vice versa*. It also regarded ASEAN as a key economic and political partner.[15]

The EU's 2004 Asia Strategy Paper sets out the framework for EU relations with Asia for 2005–06 (Europa 2004c). This paper outlines the aims to enhance existing partnerships, increase the political and economic presence of the EU within Asia, balance economic, political and socio–cultural relations, and deal with Asian states and groups as equal partners. Although it sets out relations with ASEAN, SAARC and ASEM, the most developed of these relationships are the EU–ASEAN and ASEM fora. The EU's General Affairs Council reiterated a commitment to ASEM in this context for 2004 (Europa 2004b).

In spite of numerous pledges of commitment towards Asia and a plethora of documents supporting bilateral and interregional engagements, the EU in general retains less interest in East Asia than the region's growing economic and political weight would merit. This apparent disinterest can be explained in various ways. First, the EU's own integration processes have required much time and resources. Second, there is a lack — with the exception of human rights issues in Myanmar and, to a muted extent, China — of contentious issues related to the region. Third, there are many different fora for addressing the same issues, which provide the EU with a growing set of relations with East Asia and serve "quite different and complementary purposes" (Europa 2002). The development of relations from an EU–ASEAN dialogue to the ASEM framework also offers the EU a nuanced and qualitatively different approach to the region and embody an earlier commitment to undertake "collective steps" *vis-à-vis* third countries in fields other than trade (Edwards & Regelsberger 1990, 12). This illustrates how complementary forms of interregionalism may be seen to be developing at both EU–ASEAN and EU–East Asia levels.

Bilateral Relations

When he met Chinese Prime Minister Wen Jiaobao in the Hague in December 2004 for the seventh China–EU summit, EU Commission President José Manuel Barroso observed that the development of relations with China is "one of our top foreign policy objectives in the years to come" (Europa 2004e). The summit pledged the development of a new EU–China framework on trade and investment and echoed a range of issues raised at ASEM, including EU calls for support for a Doha Development Round (Europa 2004f). The bilateral relationship complemented exchanges within ASEM by tackling specific issues, such as an agreement on tourism and satellite navigation, as well as providing the channel for opening discussions about the possible ending of the arms embargo imposed against China in 1989. It is codified in the 2001 Communication from the European Commission, Council and Parliament, entitled the "EU Strategy Towards China" (which builds on a 1998 paper) and notes the targets of supporting China's greater entry into the international community and world economy and its transition to open society, as well as raising the EU's profile in China. Observing that "China is not always an easy partner for the EU", it is clear that multi-channel approaches to Beijing serve the EU well at the present stage, by enabling a range of subjects to be tackled by different representatives (Europa 2004d).

In a similar way, the EU–Japan dialogue addresses issues such as two-way investment and the enforcement of intellectual property rights, which are dealt with in other bilateral meetings of the EU, as well as in the broader interregional framework. Based upon the 2001 Action Plan (superseding the 1991 Joint Declaration), this relationship enables Tokyo to be addressed directly through a bilateral exchange as well as through the broader forum. Thus, bilateral relations should not be regarded as a substitute for interregional endeavours, but they adopt the latter as the backdrop upon which to focus more specific discussions. Moreover, the interregional framework provides a means for the EU of promoting a regional balance between the bilateral relations of Japan and China.

Neglecting South Asia?

As illustrated above, in some ways the development of the ASEM process and ensuing strengthening of the EU–ASEAN dialogue have served to reinforce a notion of East Asia for a variety of purposes within the EU. As the number of applicants for membership to the ASEM process testifies (including India, Pakistan and Russia) and as accrued benefits to the new member states of both the EU and ASEAN would suggest, greater gaps can develop through such exclusive groups.[16]

In the case of South Asia, the development of EU–East Asian interregionalism has had two main effects. First, trade and investment priorities within ASEM and the EU–ASEAN dialogues contrast with aid and assistance programmes towards South Asia. To this end, the EU has instigated a number of institutional responses towards aiding developing parts of Asia, channelling most of its activities through the European Communities Humanitarian Office (ECHO). Moreover, in response to the effects of the December 2004 *tsunami* in Southeast and South Asia, the European Commission established a Civil Protection Mechanism to coordinate its response alongside other EU and United Nations agencies. Interestingly, in response to this crisis, Thailand and other states were determined to remind potential aid providers of their developed (not developing) country status within an apparently developed region.

Second, ASEM reinforces the template of interregionalism and the EU has attempted on a number of occasions to re-ignite relations with SAARC, while recognizing South Asia to be "distinct from the rest of Asia", given its level of development and the predominantly aid–based relationship (Europa 2004c). For example, Pakistan's GSP benefits were increased following the events of 11 September 2001, in order to facilitate development and financial reform. Moreover, the least developed countries of South Asia also benefit from the 'Everything But Arms (EBA) Regulation', which provides duty–free access to the EU market without any quantitative restrictions, except to arms and munitions. These differentiated approaches towards Southeast and South Asia suggest a continued donor–recipient format in the case of the latter but a graduated status for Southeast Asia, as part of a wider regional grouping of East Asia. In this way, the explicit nature of the region as part of an interregional framework may serve to reinforce further differences between East and South Asia.

5. Regional Identity in East Asia

Contrasting East Asia and Europe

By the time of the first ASEM, the topic of 'Europe' had been prominent in the Asian media for many years, since the fall of the Berlin Wall in 1989 and, particularly, in light of the success of the Maastricht Treaty of 1992, which pronounced the imminent arrival of the single currency. In addition, years of incremental achievements for the EC/EU, especially through the Commission with its delegations in non–EU member states, had given the EU a *de facto* international political as well as economic role that East Asia could not ignore. Throughout the late 1990s and early 2000s, the establishment by the Treaty of Amsterdam in 1997 of a High Representative within the Council of Ministers' General Secretariat (currently in the person of former NATO Secretary–General Javier Solana), the overall growth and institutionalisation of the Common Foreign and Security Policy (CFSP), the introduction of the euro and the formulation of an EU Constitution further reinforced in practice the EU's growing external presence.

These developments led to calls within East Asia for the strengthening of regional collaboration in a perceived trilateral (EU–US–East Asia) global economy and even for the creation of some kind of currency union akin to the European model. More importantly, perhaps, when it came to preparations for the first ASEM summit the (then) Asian ten had to sit down together as a group for the first time, in order to formulate responses to their European interlocutor. As the process of collaboration continued, supported by a realisation during the 1997 currency crisis that East Asia lacked the means to collectively address regional challenges, there was soon greater momentum for closer cooperation among the ASEM Asian states. The first APT meeting in 1997 represented a formal recognition of a tangible East Asian identity (Hook *et al.* 2001, 154). If it did not instigate it, the ASEM process strengthened this growing concept of East Asia as an "equal partner" to Europe (Aggarwal & Fogarty 2004).

Since its inaugural meeting, the APT has developed an elaborate structure of meetings, which now include not only an annual summit but also foreign and finance ministers' meetings, as well as specialist meetings such as the ministerial meeting on transnational crime, which met for the first time in January 2004. Since the sixth summit in November 2002, moreover, the APT has expanded its remit to address regional political and security issues, such as terrorism and non–traditional security, and now embraces many of the subjects featured on ASEM's own agenda. This may represent the "reactionary regionalism" observed by Beeson, but ASEM has certainly contributed to the creation of a notion of regional identity through the delineation of 'self' and 'other' (Beeson 2003).

Possibilities for the East Asian Region

The actual trajectory of regionness that East Asia will eventually adopt remains to be seen. Among the many options, an *oppositional* East Asia may come to regard the EU as a counter–model for integration, particularly if the so–called 'Asian values' debate accrues greater credence and Western calls for the ending of 'crony capitalism' or Asian human rights abuses continue to locate the region as a negative other. Additionally, a *partnership* East Asia may develop, representing a body of equal status to that of its European interlocutor. The possibilities for two–way regionalism as espoused through ASEM, and in contradistinction to the early years of EU–ASEAN dialogue and current EU–SAARC relationship, would suggest that this is possible, reinforced by an apparent East Asian confidence to address some of its collective concerns as a group. Even more so than is the case with 'oppositional' Asia, however, intra–regional rivalries, particularly between China and Japan, and China and Taiwan, may jeopardise the region's ability to sustain such coherence. Alternatively, a *mirror* Asia may construct its own future through participation in fora such as ASEM and in the face of a clearly definable other. In this formulation, the pursuit of greater institutional mechanisms for the formalisation of regional responses would be needed. To date, this model has been actively resisted by many East Asian participants, who would rather retain their own way of doing business than adopt Western norms wholesale (Wendt 1996, 49). At the same time, as Stubbs observes, the participation of previously disparate and usually unheard non–state actors may proliferate within interregional fora and serve to give any East Asian model of region an emphasis on social, not legal obligations (Stubbs 1998, 70). It is clear that a growing sense of regional identification is now tangible within East Asia, which increasingly presents itself in international fora as a legitimate pole of the global triad (Stubbs 1998, 68). In these ways, interregionalism is important for East Asia, not only for dealing with a growing EU, but also for enhancing the very formation of a sense of regional self.

6. Conclusion: a New Interregionalism?

The ASEM process is the newest of the interregional arrangements to be covered in this special issue, but does it represent 'new interregionalism'? As was illustrated above, it was established at a crossroads of international and regional events and builds upon historical ties across and between the continents of East Asia and Europe. In its present state, it offers a number of lessons for understanding interregionalism.

Managing Changes

First, it plays a functional role in managing global change. Interregionalism may be seen as a response to changes in the structure of the global political economy and, especially since the events of 11 September 2001, as a means of tackling trans–border threats and challenges. Such concerns also mean that issues may transcend previous categories and, for example, financial and political agenda may need to be dealt with together, as in the case of counter–terrorism. As has been illustrated above, it can serve to draw the broad canvas upon which smaller scale interaction, such as bilateral summits, can occur, by developing an ongoing agenda and a familiar pattern of terminology. This acts a as a shorthand, so that bilateral engagements can be spent on more targeted aims and focused bargaining. It is now accepted that East Asia and the EU 'matter' to one another, as trade between them has surpassed that of EU–US trade and as, during the 1980s and especially the 1990s, regional trade agreements, as opposed to global ones, became "more politically desirable and feasible due to increased familiarity and comparable cultures, business practices and legal systems" (Yeung *et al.* 1999, 20).

Role of Regions

Second, and linked to the management of change, it reinforces the role of regions as actors. Changes in the global economy and the scale of trans–border activities mean that regions have acted themselves into significance. However, those not in the interregional listings are excluded from the benefits that accrue from membership. The exclusion, not only of Australia and New Zealand, but also of indubitably 'Asian' states such as India and Pakistan, demonstrates the development of a certain kind of economically developed East Asia.[17] Assumptions about the nature of this East Asia are easily maintained, as EU Commissioner Manuel Marín noted: "We don't operate like the Americans. In our search for compromise, we work almost like the Asians" (Ton 1998). Linked to this point, the very notion of region-ness is embedded in the process of Asia–Europe interaction, as the East Asian regional self acts itself into being, in part through its acceptance as a region by the EU. This is not to argue that East Asia has solely been defined through the interregional mechanisms of ASEM, rather to suggest that the explicitly interregional process has been important in further delineating the contours of Asian regionness and in highlighting, albeit in a *post facto* manner, how processes such as the APT and regional financial initiatives have become part of a regional discourse that is most visible in its interregional iteration.

Two–Way Interregionalism

Third, the ASEM process provides the possibility for two–way inter-regionalism, whereby region–to–region processes may affect intra–regional developments themselves. Interregionalism should not be regarded simply as region–to–region dialogue, incorporating two rational actors, which are "created and recreated in the process of global transformation" as "territo-rial based subsystems of the international system" (Hettne *et al.* 1999, xv). Rather, interregionalism has the additional potential to establish a regional profile beyond one's own confines (as in the EU's search for recognition in East Asia), or affect the development of the intra–regional identity of one of its participating actors. In this way, it provides a focused and interactive self/ other nexus, by locating two regions in a situation of parity. This is also important for determining the types of region likely to emerge in the medium term, as the EU utilizes new channels to demonstrate its deepening and widening regional credentials, and as East Asian states adopt the loose regional format developed in ASEM to address a number of their intra-regional concerns.

Non–State Actors

Fourth, ASEM opens spaces for the participation of new actors. Interregionalism creates new possibilities for transcending not only the confines of the state, but also for including participants from below the level of the state, such as business, citizens and non–governmental groupings. At the same time, there remains a tension in its efforts to articulate such a space. On the one hand, the business community has been given full membership of the interregional framework within ASEM, as its members hold the key to closer economic linkages between each region. On the other, the interregional structure of ASEM has the potential to include a number of non–state actors who, as yet, lack a legitimate voice in the domestic arenas from which they come. If interregional participation enables those actors to challenge or threaten those very structures, then those states are unlikely to sanction greater NGO participation in interregional exchange.

ASEM and Interregionalism

In the case of ASEM, it is worth returning to the four principles it espouses, in order to see how and whether it offers a example of 'new interregionalism'. First, the informal nature of ASEM does bring together a range of actors who have never previously encountered one another in such a structured way. However, the scope of their discussion is broad and the consensus–based framework renders the decision–making process slow and cumbersome. Second, the multi–dimensionality of ASEM gives it the space to address a range of issues simultaneously and the potential, expressed in discussions over anti–terrorism, to advance the security remit too. In reality, however, this has yet to be developed and the breadth of issues covered in ASEM suggests it plays a greater role in disseminating information than in making decisions. Third, it enshrines the notion of 'equal partnership' in a way that the EU–ASEAN dialogue cannot, given its history and the collective (relatively low) economic and political weight of its Southeast Asian grouping. The inclusion of China, Japan and South Korea gives the notion of 'East Asia' greater weight. Finally, ASEM in some ways is hamstrung by its own high–profile expectations, as European leaders consistently fail to accord it a suitably high status. In these ways, the interregionalism of ASEM does bring something 'new' to the table, but, by its very nature, it may not always be as clear or high–profile as it could be. On the face of it, this meeting appears to contribute very little to world affairs: internal Asian disagreements over trade opening measures and debates over Asian versus Western norms on the subject of human rights leave only a hollow ring beyond their ASEM walls. Nevertheless, the strength of ASEM lies in the fact that it offers a new channel of communication with the potential to bring together state and non–state actors of two geographical regions with a history of political and economic distance.

Notes

1. 'East Asia' refers to the ASEAN Plus Three (APT) states of Brunei, Cambodia, China, Japan, Indonesia, Laos, Malaysia, Myanmar, the Philippines, Singapore, South Korea, Thailand and Vietnam.
2. The author is grateful to Fredrik Söderbaum for highlighting this issue.
3. The original ASEAN member states are Indonesia, Malaysia, the Philippines, Singapore and Thailand. Brunei Darusslam joined in 1984, Vietnam in 1995, Laos and Myanmar in 1997 and Cambodia in 1999.
4. The member states of SAARC are Bangladesh, Bhutan, India, the Maldives, Nepal, Pakistan and Sri Lanka.
5. By the end of 2004, however, the financial support part of the memorandum of understanding had still to be fulfilled.
6. The original member states of ASEM are: on the EU side, Austria, Belgium, Denmark, Finland, France, Germany, Greece, Ireland, Italy, Luxembourg, the Netherlands, Portugal, Spain, Sweden and the UK; on the Asian side, Brunei, China, Indonesia, Japan, Malaysia, the Philippines, Singapore, South Korea, Thailand and Vietnam. At ASEM 5 in 2004, thirteen new member states were admitted: the ten new member states of the EU, namely, Cyprus, the Czech Republic, Estonia, Hungary, Latvia, Lithuania, Malta, Poland, Slovakia and Slovenia; and Cambodia, Laos and Myanmar.
7. *Daily Yomiuri* (3 March 1996).
8. *The Economist* (2 March 1996).
9. *The Financial Times* (14/15 March 1998 and 27 March 1998).
10. *The Financial Times* (21/22 October 2000).
11. ASEM Chair's Statement, Seoul 2000.
12. Further information is available at http://www.asef.org (accessed 12 May 2005).
13. The EP has made *causes célèbres* and issued resolutions with regard to particular issues, such as human rights' abuses in Myanmar/Burma (for instance, 22 October 1996, 16 September 1999, 18 May 2000, 7 September 2000), and has urged the European Commission and Common Foreign and Security Policy High Representative to make a determined effort to visit Mrs Aung San Suu Kyi and for the EU and its member states to implement economic sanctions against Burma.
14. *Europe Documents* (12 October 1995); *Daily Yomiuri* (27 February 1996).
15. The central role of ASEAN was further recognized in the July 2003 European Commission Communication entitled 'A New Partnership with South East Asia'.
16. ASEM has a principle of inclusivity, but each region has to agree to the admission of any new members.
17. *Asian Wall Street Journal* (23 February 1996).

References

Aggarwal, V. K. & Fogarty E. A. (eds) (2004) *EU Trade Strategies: Between Regionalism and Globalism* (Basingstoke: Palgrave Macmillan).

Beeson, M. (2003) ASEAN Plus Three and the Rise of Reactionary Regionalism, Available at: http://eprint.uq.edu.au/archive/00000496/01/mbasean03.pdf (accessed 13 September 2004).

Campbell, D. (1998, 1992) *Writing Security: United States Foreign Policy and the Politics of Identity* (Manchester: Manchester University Press).

Camroux, D. & Lechervy, C. (1996) "Close Encounter of a Third Kind?": The Inaugural Asia–Europe Meeting of March 1996, *The Pacific Review* 9(3), pp. 442–453.

Chan, J. (1998) Asian values and human rights: an alternative view, in: L. Diamond & M. F. Platter (eds) *Democracy in East Asia*, pp. 28–41 (Baltimore: Johns Hopkins University Press).

Colbert, E. (1992) Southeast Asian Regional Politics: Toward a Regional Order, in: W. Howard Wriggins (ed.) *Dynamics of Regional Politics: 4 Systems on the Indian Ocean Rim*, pp. 213–273 (New York: Columbia University Press).

CAEC: Council for Asia–Europe Cooperation Paris Plenary Meeting (1996) Informal Summary, November, available at: http://www.jcie.or.jp/thinknet/caec/paris96.html (accessed 1 July 1999).

Dent, C. (1999) The EU–East Asia Relationship: The Persisting Weak Triadic Link?, *European Foreign Affairs Review* 4(3), pp. 371–394.

Dixon, C. (1991) *South East Asia in the World–Economy* (Cambridge: Cambridge University Press).

Edwards, G. & Regelsberger, E. (eds) (1990) *Europe's Global Links* (London: Pinter).

Europa (2002) http://www.europa.eu.int/comm/external_relations/news/patten/sp02_368.htm (accessed 31 December 2004).

Europa (2004a) http://europa.eu.int/comm/external_relations/asean/intro (accessed 31 December 2004).

Europa (2004b) http://www.europa.eu.int/comm/external_relations/asem/gac.htm (accessed 31 December 2004).

Europa (2004c) http://www.europa.eu.int/comm/external_relations/asia/rsp/rsp.asia.pdf (accessed 31 December 2004).

Europa (2004d) http://www.europa.eu.int/comm/external_relations/china/com01_265.pdf (accessed 31 December 2004).

Europa (2004e) http://www.europa.eu.int/comm/external_relations/china/summit_1204_1440.htm (accessed 31 December 2004).

Europa (2004f) http://www.europa.eu.int/comm/external_relations/news/barroso/sp04_523.htm (accessed 30 November 2004).

European Commission (2000) Perspectives and Priorities for the ASEM Process (Asia–Europe Meeting) into the New Decade, COM 2000 (241), 18 April.

Finger, M. (1994) NGOs and Transformation: Beyond Social Movement Theory, in: T. Princen & M. Finger (eds) *Environmental NGOs in World Politics*, pp. 48–66 (London: Routledge).

Gamble, A. & Payne, A. (eds) (1996) *Regionalism and World Order* (London: Macmillan).

Gilson, J. (2002) *Asia Meets Europe: Interregionalism and the Asia–Europe Meeting* (Cheltenham: Edward Elgar).

Hettne, B., Inotai, A. & Sunkel, O. (eds) (1999) *Globalism and the New Regionalism* (London: Macmillan).

Higgott, R. (1994) Ideas, Interests and Identity in the Asia Pacific, *The Pacific Review*, 7(4), pp. 367–380.

Hook, G., Gilson, J., Hughes, C. W. & Dobson, H. (2001) (second edition, 2005), *Japan's International Relations* (London: Routledge).

Kumar, A. (2004) EU–South Asia relations in trade and investment, 11 May, available at: http://www.ased.org/artman/publish/printer_598.shtml (accessed 12 November 2004).

Lach, D. (1965) *Asia in the Making of Europe*, Vol. I. (Chicago and London: University of Chicago Press).

Maull, H., Wanandi, J. & Segal, G. (eds) (1998) *Europe and the Asia Pacific* (London and New York: Routledge).

MOFA (Japanese Ministry of Foreign Affairs) (2004), http://www.mofa.go.jp/mofaj/area/asem/asem6_gh_sengen_e.html (accessed 12 November 2004).

Patten, C. (2002) Speech made on 6 September, available at: http://www.europa.eu.int/comm/external_relations/news/patten/sp02_368.htm (accessed 31 December 2004).

Pou Serradell, V. (1996) The Asia–Europe meeting (ASEM): A Historical Turning Point in Relations between the Two Regions, *European Foreign Affairs Review* 1(2), pp. 185–210.

Princen, T. (1994) NGOs: Creating a Niche in Environmental Diplomacy, in: T. Princen & M. Finger (eds) *Environmental NGOs in World Politics*, pp. 29–47 (London: Routledge).

Richards, G. (2000) ASEM and the New Politics of Development. Paper presented to the 'Trade and Economy Forum', ASEM People's Forum, Seoul, 18–19 October.

Sampson, E. E. (1993) *Celebrating the Other: A Dialogic Account of Human Nature* (New York: Harvester Wheatsheaf).

SarDesai, D.R. (1997) *Southeast Asia: Past and Present* (Boulder: Westview Press).

Scholte, J. A. (1996) Globalisation and Collective Identities, in: J. Krause & N. Renwick (eds) *Identities in International Relations*, pp. 38–78 (London: Macmillan).

Scholte, J. A. (2000) Cautionary Reflections on Seattle, *Millennium* 29(1), pp. 115–122.

Schmit, L. (1996) The Deployment of Civil Energy in Indonesia, in: C. Hann & E. Dunn (eds) *Civil Society: Challenging Western Models*, pp. 178–198 (London: Routledge).

Searle, J. R. (1995) *The Constitution of Social Reality* (London: Penguin).

Shin, D.-I. & Segal, G. (1997) Getting Serious About Asia–Europe Security Cooperation, *Survival* 39(1), pp. 139–155.

Smith, H. (1998) Korea, in: R. H. McLeod & R. Garnaut (eds) *East Asia in Crisis: From Being a Miracle to Needing One?*, pp. 66–84 (London: Routledge).

Stubbs, R. (1998) Asia–Pacific Regionalism versus Globalization, in W. D. Coleman & G. R. D. Underhill (eds), *Regionalism and Global Economic Integration: Europe, Asia and the Americas,* pp. 68–80 (London: Routledge).

Ton Sinh Thanh (1998) The Asia–Europe Meeting: ASEAN and EU Perspectives. Paper presented to Carleton University, Ottawa, April.

Vietnam Gateway (2005) http://www.vietnamgateway.organisation/asem/news6.html (accessed 4 January 2005).

Wendt, A. (1994) Collective Identity Formation and the International State, *American Political Science Review* 88(2), pp. 384–396.

Wendt, A. (1996) Identity and Structural Change in International Politics, in: M. T. Yeung, N. Perdikis & W. A. Kerr (1999) *q.v.*

Yeung, M.T., Perdikis, N. & W. A. Kerr (eds) (1999), *Regional Trading Blocs in the Global Economy* (Cheltenham: Edward Elgar).

The Limits of Interregionalism: The EU and North America

VINOD K. AGGARWAL & EDWARD A. FOGARTY

1. Introduction

The European Union is the patron saint of interregionalism in international economic relations. It has pursued interregional strategies in one form or another toward regional groupings in South America, East Asia, the Southern Mediterranean, Eastern Europe and a variety of least–developed countries. However, the case of EU relations with North America (the United States, Canada and Mexico) shows the limits of this strategy. During the 1990s, the foundations for a transatlantic interregional relationship emerged. The EU institutionalised cooperative economic relations with the United States and Canada within separate but similar bilateral frameworks, and completed a free trade agreement (FTA) with Mexico. During the same period, the creation of the North American Free Trade Agreement (NAFTA) established a free trade zone among the more than 400 million inhabitants of North America. These developments potentially opened the door to the grandest of interregional agreements between the world's two largest regional blocs.

Yet, even as the EU pursued interregional strategies toward many other ill-defined and weakly institutionalised 'regions', it avoided an interregional approach toward its most important commercial partner. Simply put, there is no discernable EU–North America relationship. But this state of affairs is precisely what makes this case important to explore; it is just as essential to account for why interregionalism does *not* occur as it is to understand why it does.

In this case study, the past practice and future prospects of EU interregionalism toward North America in their commercial relations is viewed through an analytical lens developed by the authors elsewhere (Aggarwal & Fogarty 2004). Notably, interregionalism is not addressed as a process or outcome, as Söderbaum and van Langenhove do in the Introduction to this collection — though the authors of this piece certainly acknowledge the utility of doing so.[1] Rather, interregionalism is analysed as a policy strategy — the choice to pursue (or not to pursue, in the EU–North America case) formalised intergovernmental relations across distinct regions. Hence this study focuses on the question of why European Union policy–makers chose to pursue a policy to deal with each of the three countries of North America bilaterally, without seriously considering an interregional relationship with NAFTA.

As with any study of foreign economic policy, a variety of factors may be relevant in explaining the absence of EU interregionalism in this case. Accordingly, three 'lenses' through which to view EU commercial policy toward North America are considered: interest group preferences and behaviour, security competition, and transnational identity formation. These lenses are neither exhaustive nor mutually exclusive, but are useful tools for separating out what the authors of this study believe to be the key dynamics relevant to this case.[2] Analysis of the case through these lenses shows that there is no obvious rationale for an interregional strategy in this context, making its absence unsurprising.

In section three of this study, each analytical lens is briefly introduced in general terms, and then applied to EU commercial policy toward North America. But first EU commercial relations with each of the countries of North America and NAFTA collectively over the past fifteen years are briefly sketched to provide some empirical background for the ensuing analysis of EU commercial policy and the absence of interregionalism.

2. Describing EU Commercial Relations with North America[3]

Despite the creation of NAFTA in 1994, the EU has studiously maintained separate bilateral tracks for managing its commercial relations with the three countries of North America. Thus, to assess the EU's trade ties to NAFTA as a whole, those with each North American country individually are first considered briefly.

Europe and the United States

The Europe–United States commercial relationship remains the cornerstone of the international economy. The EU and United States represent the world's two largest markets, and each absorbs roughly 20 per cent of the other's exports, with total trade in 2002 worth roughly 650 billion USD. The relationship is similarly intimate with respect to investment: in 2001, European firms accounted for over 60 per cent of FDI stock in the United States (roughly 870 USD billion in total), while American firms owned a similar proportion of investment stock (approximately 630 billion USD in total) in EU member countries (European Commission 2003). Much of transatlantic exchange is intra–firm, underscoring the fact that this 'trade' is very much intertwined with investment and merger and acquisition activities.

During the 1990s, in the wake of the Cold War and in a period of ascendant regionalism (including in both Europe and North America), the United States and Europe struggled to recast their relations in the absence of the Soviet threat. Many analysts predicted the future of international competition to be in the field of economics rather than security, and policy–makers in the United States and Europe sought ways to retain their role as partners even as they competed commercially. Accordingly, the United States and Europe announced a series of agreements during the 1990s that attempted to institutionalise economic cooperation, with varying degrees of significance and success.

In 1990, the two sides announced a Transatlantic Declaration that was intended to deepen and institutionalise commercial relations. However, this declaration was more symbolic than substantive. Its main functional purpose was to establish a framework for regular consultation, specifically a regimen of biannual summits at which US and European ministers and heads of state would meet to discuss important issues on the transatlantic and world agendas.

The EU and United States unveiled a New Transatlantic Agenda (NTA) in December 1995 to provide some of the substance that the Transatlantic Declaration lacked. The NTA sought to broaden the scope of EU–US cooperation both on trade and investment matters as well as on transnational issues such as terrorism and the environment. On the economic front, the NTA spawned two further acronyms: the New Transatlantic Marketplace (NTM) and the Transatlantic Business Dialogue (TABD). The NTM was to be a framework for dismantling most remaining trade and investment barriers between the two, and a building block toward a possible Transatlantic Free Trade Area; but the NTM's broad agenda proved difficult to translate into specific commitments, and the NTM ultimately gave way to a somewhat less ambitious Transatlantic Economic Partnership (TEP) in 1998. The TEP focused on the mundane but important matters of harmonising standards and cooperating on non–tariff barriers more generally.

The TABD provided a forum for European and US business leaders and trade officials to generate their own agenda and momentum for closer commercial ties across the Atlantic. Indeed, the recommendations of those working within the TABD were a major factor in the push to harmonise regulations and standards. A direct result was the set of six Mutual Recognition Agreements (MRAs) signed by the United States and the EU in June 1997, which streamlined testing and approval procedures in several sectors.

Despite this alphabet soup of frameworks, no comprehensive 'meeting of the minds' has been achieved by political leaders on the future shape of transatlantic economic relations, and plenty of disagreement remains between the two on their visions for the broader international economy. Indeed, the initial failure to launch a new round of multilateral trade negotiations in Seattle in 1999 was more a result of the inability of the United States and Europe to cooperate than any protest activities on the streets (Fogarty 2005). Subsequent trade spats have clogged both the newspaper headlines and World Trade Organisation (WTO) arbitration mechanisms, most recently regarding subsidies to Airbus and Boeing, though nearly all have ultimately ended in compromise. More recent ructions resulting from disagreements over Iraq and multilateral cooperation more generally have clouded perceptions of the West as both an emotive and practical entity, making ideas of formal economic integration — which would be as much a political as an economic process — that much more distant.

The European Union and Canada

The recent trajectory of EU–Canada commercial relations has broadly followed that of EU–US relations. This fact comes as little surprise: given the broad political and economic similarities (in nature, if not size) between North America's two more economically advanced countries, the EU effectively put institutional developments in these two relationships on parallel tracks. Canada — always eager to step out of the shadow of its overweening neighbour to the south, and dependent on the EU as its second largest trading partner — has not always championed this parallelism, but has yet to prevail on the EU to take seriously any new approach to EU–Canadian relations.

During the 1990s, the EU established a set of commercial fora with Canada nearly identical to those it created with the United States. A 1990 joint declaration inaugurated biannual Europe–Canada summit meetings, which ultimately led to the agreements of the 1996 EU–Canada Action Plan to erect a framework for bilateral relations and the 1998 EU–Canada Trade Initiative (ECTI) to enhance bilateral cooperation on multilateral issues, as well as to the Canada–Europe Roundtable (CERT), a business–led forum similar to the TABD.[4] The EU and Canada also negotiated more specific agreements on customs cooperation in 1997, MRAs in 1998, and competition law enforcement in 1999.

This broad parallel to the EU–US approach occurred despite Ottawa's various attempts to pursue a separate path in EU–Canadian relations. While Canada and the United States share many structural similarities as well as common positions in several quarrels with the Europeans — notably on genetically–modified food and hormone–treated beef — Canada has its own interests to look after in its ties to Europe. While commercial relations are mostly harmonious, the EU and Canada have had several ugly confrontations over fishing rights off Canada's eastern coast. On the positive side, Canada has sought to enhance its commercial relationship with the EU to diversify its foreign trade portfolio, which at present is massively dependent on the US market — fully 86 per cent of Canadian exports go to the United States.[5]

Canada has occasionally sought to embed EU–Canadian relations in a broader EU–North America context, styling itself a facilitating middleman in a putative interregional relationship between the EU and NAFTA. The government of Jean Chrétien, the long–serving former Prime Minister of Canada, sought repeatedly in the mid to late 1990s to convince European leaders of the merits of a more interregional approach. In 1998, Canada's Minister of Trade, Sergio Marchi, envisioned a time "when Europe looks to North America [and] sees a NAFTA community, not just three different neighborhoods" (Council of Europe 2000).

Yet Canada's entreaties have been largely ignored by both Commission and European national officials.[6] However, the British government did give support to a specific EU–NAFTA track: in a February 2001 speech to the Canadian parliament, British Prime Minister Tony Blair declared the need for a "political declaration of intent" between the EU and NAFTA (Blair 2001). It is not clear, however, whether Blair's statement was intended to give impetus to an interregional EU–NAFTA track, to merge the EU–North American agendas in the run–up to WTO negotiations in Doha later that year, or simply to humour the Canadian government. Either way, EU policy–makers have shown little inclination to make Canada the key to their North American strategy.

The European Union and Mexico

In the years up to the 1990s, Mexico was peripheral to European commercial strategy, as it accounted for less than one per cent of Europe's international trade. However, as the EU commercial agenda began to place greater emphasis on increasing trade with less–developed countries, and as the United States moved toward a free–trade agreement with Mexico, European perceptions began to change. The completion of NAFTA posed an immediate problem for the European Union: it weakened Europe's position in a liberalising and potentially dynamic Mexico, Latin America's second largest market and home to nearly 100 million consumers. These fears were warranted: Europe saw its share of Mexican trade drop from more than 9 per cent in 1993 to 6 per cent in 2000. Meanwhile, the US totals jumped 5 per cent (to a more than 80 per cent share) over the same period (European Commission 2000). While these trends were clearly in place before NAFTA, it promised to worsen the EU's terms of trade with Mexico, and thus further marginalise European exporters in that market.

The EU's response was to initiate and, in 1999, to complete, a bilateral free trade area with Mexico. The free trade agreement, known officially as the 'Economic Partnership, Political Coordination and Cooperation Agreement', or more grandiloquently as the 'Global Agreement', has been referred to by Pascal Lamy as "in terms of coverage the most ambitious free trade agreement ever negotiated by the EU" (European Commission 2000). Specifically, the Global Agreement set hard targets for complete liberalisation of trade in industrial goods (the EU by 1 January 2003; Mexico by 1 January 2007) and broad liberalisation of agriculture (by 2010, 80 per cent of EU imports and 42 per cent of Mexican imports) and fisheries (by 2010, 100 per cent of EU imports and 89 per cent of Mexican imports). It also granted Mexico preferential treatment in the services sector, while further liberalising government procurement, investment, competition and intellectual property policies. Institutionally, it established a Joint Council, which meets at the ministerial level to uphold the Global Agreement's 'pillars' of political dialogue, trade liberalisation and general cooperation, and which maintains a dispute settlement mechanism should disagreements arise.

Like the EU, which sought a free trade area with Mexico in large part to redress the deterioration of its terms of trade after the creation of NAFTA, Mexico's broad motivations for pursuing a deal with Europe are not difficult to divine. Like Canada during the 1980s and (especially) 1990s, Mexico saw its trade dependence on the United States grow to staggering levels: in 1982, Mexico sent 53 per cent of its total exports north of the border; by 1999 that number had ballooned to 90 per cent (Gower 2000). The Mexican government's liberalisation policies over this period had increased the proportion of the economy dependent on international trade, thereby intensifying Mexico's vulnerability to economic shocks in the United States. Thus it had every reason to seek to diversify its trade relationships — and particularly to embrace Europe, a market very similar in size and purchasing power to that of the United States. Mexico's desire to reduce its dependency on its northern neighbour became more salient with the US administration's post–9/11 dismissal of Mexican initiatives to deepen NAFTA through additional agreements on aid and immigration. Europe, in 1982, absorbed over 20 per cent of Mexican exports — a proportion that had fallen to just 3.1 per cent in 1999 (Gower 2000) — so perhaps a free–trade deal that evened out the playing field *vis–à–vis* NAFTA would re–establish the vitality of this trade relationship, something both the EU and Mexico were keen to encourage.

The European Union and NAFTA

Describing the relationship between the EU and NAFTA is not a straightforward task, for the simple reason that it does not officially exist. However, it is possible to consider some aspects of NAFTA relevant to a prospective interregional relationship.

The main hindrance to EU–North American commerce — and the issue addressed in agreements like the MRAs — is non–tariff barriers such as subsidies and product standards. The primacy that technical issues such as NTBs now take in EU–North American trade relations underscores how deeply integrated the two sides' economies already are. The EU accounts for 35 per cent of NAFTA's exports (excluding intra–North American trade) and 25 per cent of its imports, and thus is NAFTA's most important trading partner. Together, the EU and NAFTA account for 35 per cent of world exports and over 40 per cent of world imports, making the transatlantic link not only central to each side's economies, but to the international economy as a whole (DTI 2001). What happens in transatlantic economic relations — in official trade agreements or disputes, as well as in day–to–day commercial transactions — has repercussions far beyond the arena in which they are governed. Whether and how an EU–NAFTA relationship was to develop would affect every other trade regime in the world, from bilateral and regional groupings to the WTO itself.

The future of EU–North American interregionalism may be broadly constrained by two aspects of NAFTA's organisational form: its institutionalisation and its asymmetry. While NAFTA is highly institutionalised — featuring a clear set of rules governing trade and investment, provisions to ensure the integrity of labour and environmental standards, and a dispute settlement mechanism for managing conflict — it is minimally integrationist. Born of the convergence of pragmatic self–interest among its members, NAFTA is unlikely to develop into an economic union or customs union in the absence of a major shift in the international political and economic climate — and, more importantly, the US domestic political climate.[7]

The overwhelmingly dominant position of the United States within NAFTA and the consistent scepticism of the US Congress to most types of international economic integration constitute a hard ceiling to NAFTA's evolution. Unlike Europe, where a fairly even distribution of power among the largest member states (and within the traditional Franco–German axis) has fostered a political environment of multilateralism and consensus, the hegemony of the United States and deep, asymmetrical dependence of Canada and Mexico on the US economy place the fate of NAFTA essentially in the relationship between the US administration and the Congress. While Congress finally granted the President 'trade promotion authority' in the summer of 2002 (eight years after it had elapsed), its hostility to further international trade agreements after the completion of NAFTA and the Uruguay Round of the GATT has slowed US participation in trade negotiations at all levels. Hence Canada's lonely calls for closer EU–NAFTA relations, and Mexico's hopes for greater intra–NAFTA integration, will both go unheeded unless political conditions change dramatically in the United States.

Moreover, NAFTA may ultimately be a transitional arrangement, intended more as a building block toward hemispheric free trade than an end in itself. This state of affairs seems clear from Washington's negotiating tactics, which have involved signing bilateral free trade agreements with individual South American countries and an FTA with countries from Central

America before the creation of a transregional Free Trade Area of the Americas (FTAA), thus strengthening a US–friendly NAFTA model over a more developmentalist version preferred by Brazil and some other Latin American countries. This potentially transitional character of NAFTA means that it is unlikely to take on any greater integrationist elements among current and/or future members; negotiations among all the countries of the hemisphere toward anything but a straight free trade area — as opposed to, say, a customs union — would be far too difficult to manage within the proposed time frame (negotiations for an FTAA are supposed to be completed in 2005). In short, while the unresolved shape of NAFTA is not, in itself, a barrier to an interregional arrangement with the EU — after all, the EU itself is constantly evolving in both membership and structure — North and South American as well as European policy–makers' perceptions of its temporary character are. Only if the FTAA were to founder would NAFTA be likely to take on a more permanent status and potentially make separate interregional agreements on its own.[8]

Compared to its relations with other regional groupings around the world, the EU has shown little inclination to engage NAFTA collectively as a means to promote a regionalist model of economic organisation.[9] Even if the EU did want to promote greater internal coherence in NAFTA, however, significant obstacles stand in the way. As Alberta Sbragia has indicated, the EU and NAFTA are not "institutionally compatible entities" — the EU being an economic/monetary union, NAFTA a mere trade/investment union — and thus NAFTA does not have any executive with the external negotiating authority similar to the Commission (Sbragia 2001). While in some cases of interregional relations the EU literally created its counterpart region, NAFTA already exists and will evolve only to the extent that Washington allows; there would be no diffusion of institutional forms from the EU to NAFTA in the way that there might be among regions that aspire to EU–like structures. Even if interregional negotiations were to begin, a transatlantic free trade area would be a discussion between Brussels and Washington. As one British parliamentarian has remarked, "When politicians in Europe talk about 'transatlantic,' they really mean the United States of America. This is an extremely important point that Canadians and Mexicans need to appreciate" (Council of Europe 2000, 17–18). While this situation of institutional incompatibility does not rule out progress in EU–NAFTA relations, it does imply that convergence between the two would remain limited.

3. Explaining the Absence of EU Interregional Strategies Toward North America

But NAFTA's limitations do not explain EU strategy; EU–centred factors do. Hence three hypotheses are considered as potential explanations for the absence of an EU interregional strategy toward North America: interest group preferences, great power politics, and EU identity–building processes. These standard hypotheses of foreign economic policy preference and strategy formation are used as lenses through which to view different influences on EU policy in relative isolation from one another; none is a full and accurate description of events in and of itself. Rather, individually and collectively these lenses demonstrate that the absence of an EU interregional strategy toward North America is entirely unsurprising, because few of the conditions necessary for adoption of such a strategy are present.

Interest Groups

Our first lens focuses on the role of interest groups. In this 'pluralist' view, European Union commercial policy results from the capture of the EU policy–making apparatus by societal interests (i.e., firms, industry associations, environmental groups, etc.) that promote policies reflecting their particular preferences.[10] What concerns us most here is not the question of group mobilisation but rather the nature of interest group preferences: which European groups and/or sectors would support an interregional strategy and why?[11]

For European commercial sectors in particular, the question regarding economic relations with North America is: what do they want that they do not already have?[12] Though private European actors have vital interests at stake in North America, does the somewhat unsettled state of official relations serve as a strong enough incentive for them to demand a more formal interregional relationship?

Some European sectors — such as financial services, environmental technologies and knowledge–based industries — are well disposed toward free trade in general due to their relative competitiveness in international markets. Many of these same industries are particularly interested in maintaining free access to North American markets because their interests there are intra–firm. The acceleration in mergers and acquisitions (M&A) activity has created a set of multinational enterprises such as DaimlerChrysler and the Virgin Group that form a truly transatlantic constituency and which would have much to lose if any sort of trade war were to break out. Many of these and other free trade–oriented firms have been active in the business–led fora of the TABD and the CERT, and were important players behind the Mutual Recognition Agreements the EU signed with the United States and Canada in 1998 (Council of Europe 2000, 6). Indeed, the Commission is explicitly solicitous of business group advocacy: Lamy, addressing a meeting of the TABD, asked business leaders to "keep the pressure on us" for continued transatlantic liberalisation (Lamy 1999a). If sporadic conflicts with the United States continue, previously unmobilised industries might increase the pressure on the EU to find new ways to settle these issues.

Moreover, NAFTA's rules of origin have generated new incentives for European exporters to seek more direct access to North American markets. Some have suggested that the Global Agreement was just a way for European firms to get better access to the US market, making Mexico "a gateway rather than a destination," a "springboard into the United States" (Gower 2000, 3–4). So why not push for a deal that cuts out the middleman? Would European firms not prefer a straight deal with the United States, or all of

NAFTA, given the maze of rules of origin of provisions that NAFTA set up to try to clog this gateway? A formal EU–NAFTA economic partnership would certainly be a forum to clear this hindrance and facilitate European producers' access to all of North America.

Arrayed against this set of pro–free–trade groups and their liberalising incentives are a number of politically influential sectors that are more sceptical about any moves toward trade liberalisation with North America. Some of these sectors — such as textiles, steel and, of course, agriculture — were mollified in the context of the EU–Mexico free trade agreement because it gave them generous adjustment periods. The date for Europe's removal of trade barriers in the agricultural and fisheries areas (2010) comes well after the expected completion of the Millennium Round of WTO negotiations, which should force the EU to open these sectors to greater international competition anyway. However, certain sectoral sticking points with the United States and Canada — with whom trade is generally free but for which no comprehensive formal agreement exists — would arouse more opposition within Europe. In particular, EU–Canadian sensitivities on fisheries remain raw, and attempts by the Commission to rein in the EU fleet have met stiff opposition, particularly from the Spanish.[13] Meanwhile, the United States and Canada have protested at EU restrictions on their exports of hormone–treated beef and other genetically modified food products, and it is hard to see EU farmers — and perhaps consumers as well — accepting compromise on this issue.[14] More generally, recent additions to traditional safeguards — including huge increases in farm supports in the United States and a Franco–German agreement to retain CAP funds even in the face of EU enlargement — seem to make any agreement that actually reduces supports a distant dream.

Other problem sectors might not be quite as intractable. For instance, the EU shares a common position on textiles liberalisation with the United States, Canada and Mexico (along with Turkey, an EU aspirant), with all resisting the demands of India and other developing countries that they make concessions in WTO negotiations beyond those agreed in the Agreement on Textiles and Clothing, which lapses in 2005. Meanwhile, the row over the Bush administration's imposition in 2002 of temporary tariffs on steel imports (from which Canada and Mexico were notably exempted) died down as Washington waived restrictions on an ever–growing proportion of imports. Still, a surge in US protection in several industries sensitive in both North America and Europe is unlikely to put European producers in the mood to accept a rollback in their own protection.

Given the relative parity among European free–trade groups and their more sceptical counterparts, and the relative acceptability (and intractability) of the status quo for all involved, there has not been — and seems to be little prospect of — an interest group–led groundswell for an interregional strategy toward North America. On balance, an interregional agreement might be a moderate improvement on the status quo, but the limited gains of such an agreement compare unfavourably with the costs of a broad–based business mobilisation for such an outcome — especially because individual industries seem more interested in sector–specific agreements than in broader ones in which their goals might be negotiated away.[15] In this environment, the preferences of the sceptics hold sway.

Great Power Politics

Our second lens focuses on the role of international power politics. From this 'realist' perspective, the EU uses its foreign economic policy to promote European political and economic influence and security within the international system. Indeed, as long as Europe remains primarily a 'civilian power', commercial policy is its most effective means of exercising international influence.

In this context, a general interregional commercial strategy could extend European influence via a series of 'hegemon–centred' commercial agreements with regions that may or may not have significant ties amongst themselves.[16] In most region–to–region relationships, the European Union is the dominant side, and thus can largely dictate the terms of these institutionalised relationships. However, this condition does not apply in the case of North America, which is home to the EU's main commercial rival, the United States.

The imperatives of power politics do not imply overt security competition with the United States, nor do they necessarily preclude a transatlantic interregionalism. European policy–makers understand that trade is not zero–sum, and that a trade war with the United States would leave both worse off. Thus an EU trade strategy toward North America that engaged the United States in an agreement — whether multilateral, interregional or bilateral — whose terms reflected the interests of Europe more than those of the United States would provide relative gains. However, EU policy–makers have few illusions about the likelihood of such a deal, and thus have pursued their relative gains elsewhere — namely by engaging other countries and regions to promote European economic interests at the expense of their American competitors.

Such a strategy seems evident in the European approach to the Americas and East Asia. The EU's interregional negotiations with Mercosur have been driven in large part by the spectre of a future FTAA. That is, deals with Latin America are not only part of a proactive strategy to maximise Europe's influence and market access but, rather, a reaction to similar American initiatives in the region.[17] Similar positional considerations were also important in the EU's pursuit of interregional ties with an even more strategically important region, East Asia. Europeans reacted with some dismay to the coming–of–age of the US–led Asia–Pacific Economic Cooperation (APEC) forum in 1993–94, which threatened to privilege US trade with this dynamic region at the expense of an emerging Eurasian relationship. The European response was to sponsor, in 1996, the creation of the Asia–Europe Meetings (ASEM), which promised to promote and institutionalise commercial ties along this relatively underdeveloped third leg of international economic relations. It is notable that ASEM's forward momentum slowed nearly simultaneously with the deceleration of the APEC process.[18] The more general point is that, like the United States, the EU appears to be not only hedging its bets in the face of the possible breakdown of multilateral liberalisation through the WTO, but also seeking to improve relative access to key developing country markets.

Perhaps paradoxically, a central assumption underpinning this sort of 'geoeconomic' thinking is the continued stability of the transatlantic relationship itself. But what if this assumption were false — what if the vitality of EU–US political and economic relationship were fundamentally challenged by either internal dissention (e.g., the cumulative weight of successive trade–related disagreements, or the collapse of NATO), or if a credible external threat to Western civilization were to arise? In any of these scenarios might we expect EU (and US) policy–makers to reaffirm and strengthen the transatlantic link through formal commercial integration? The answer probably remains no, because doing so could generate powerful fears that the West was turning its back on the rest of the world, a decision that European and American policy–makers would have difficulty contemplating, even under the most dire circumstances, given its wide–ranging implications. Hunkering down in a North Atlantic bunker in reaction to global turmoil would suggest EU acquiescence in the creation of civilizational fault lines — a damaging perception, even if it were only a perception. Even during the darkest days of the Cold War, when it actually seemed possible that the West might stand alone against a hostile world, no serious steps toward formal transatlantic economic integration were taken. Such steps seem even less likely in the post–9/11 world, despite the fact that the West as a whole is a target of global terrorist networks. While these scenarios are merely counterfactual speculations, they do suggest that there is little strategic reason for the creation of a transatlantic free trade area, whether under current conditions or in the foreseeable future.

Transatlantic Identities, Convergent or Divergent

Our third lens focuses on the role of European identity–building in explaining the absence of interregionalism in EU commercial policy toward North America. In this view, European elites — particularly within the Commission but also in member countries — promote commercial strategies that might help generate notions of pan–European interests and identity among the peoples of Europe. While hardly central to Europeans' everyday lives in the same way as, for example, the introduction of the euro, an interregional commercial strategy would be a subtle way for EU policy–makers to encourage them to view themselves as part of a cohesive economic, political, and social unit that interacts with other, similar units around the world.[19]

The identity–related implications of interregionalism toward North America would be different from those of EU relations with other regions. The United States and Canada are uniquely similar societies to Europe, and thus this relationship involves association with a 'peer' region rather than one that has a clearly distinct set of cultural values and traditions, level of development, and so on. This inherent cultural closeness binds EU leaders' perceptions of commercial relations with North America to their view of the EU's place within 'the West'. Hence while some EU policy–makers might see the EU's place as the natural counterpart to North America within a vibrant Western civilization, others might see the ties of the West as a constraint on the establishment of a distinct European polity. It follows that, given the cultural content of trade and investment, the perceived utility of an interregional commercial strategy toward North America is a function of whether European policy–makers believe such a strategy promotes their vision of what the European Union is and should be.

On the one hand, European policy–makers intent on maintaining strong cultural and political ties between Europe and North America might promote North Atlantic interregionalism as a new means to bind the two sides of the Atlantic together. The EU accession in 2004 of ten countries from central and southern Europe may have tilted the balance in the Union back to those who desire close ties to the United States for cultural as well as economic, political and security reasons.[20] Moreover, Britain, which shares strong cultural affinities with Europe, the United States and Canada, has been warmest toward transatlantic interregionalism. This British position gained significant leverage over EU commercial policy when Peter Mandelson, a Briton who is interested in resurrecting the NTM, became the EU Trade Commissioner in the latter half of 2004.

Moreover, shared difficulties in coping with 'Islam' writ large may be a catalyst for a resuscitation of the West. Despite evidence that the 11 September 2001 terrorist attacks did not significantly reinvigorate US and European elites' fading sense of common cultural bonds, if Europe were to suffer attacks of similar scale from Islamic fundamentalist groups, transatlantic solidarity might dig deeper roots with a growing perception that the assaults were not just anti–American but fundamentally anti–Western.[21] Likewise, difficulties in integrating Muslim immigrants and the debate over Turkish membership in the EU might revive a shared perception of Christianity's role in defining Europe and the West. These negative associations with Islam could lead to the convergence of transatlantic identities and interests through the emerging perception of a shared 'other', making closer economic as well as political and security ties with North America an objective for EU policy–makers.

However, the more prominent trend among Europeans in recent years has been the exploration of cultural differences between Europe and the United States in particular. European elites have increasingly found common ground amongst themselves in denouncing various practices and institutions that they see as endemic to an alien American character, including the death penalty, violent crime and income inequality, among others. These views may be connected to scepticism about globalisation, which many Europeans see as an American–driven phenomenon that threatens their relatively generous welfare states — a social model that continues to defy the Americans' 'sink or swim' model.[22]

Thus, to EU policy–makers seeking a common European identity, embracing an interregional strategy toward a US–dominated North America would mean forgoing the gains of identifying the United States, in particular, as a useful 'other'.[23] As such, leaders most committed to European unity and autonomy may find it expedient to unite Europe by trumpeting European values as superior to their American counterparts.[24] However, this approach clearly has its limits. European policy–makers as a whole are careful to reiterate their support for the transatlantic relationship, and would presumably consider irreparable transatlantic estrangement far too high a price to pay for unclear gains in European identification.

Perhaps less problematically, EU policy–makers' transatlantic strategies also reflect their ongoing construction of the EU's 'international identity' — and how that international identity stands in contrast to that of the United States.[25] As Robert Kagan described the contrast between the two, the EU, born of cooperative multilateralism, seeks a "self–contained world of laws and rules based on transnational negotiation and cooperation", while the United States believes that "international laws and rules are unreliable" and "true security and the promotion of a liberal order still depend on the possession and use of military might" (Kagan 2003, 3). The Europeans' legalistic approach to international relations seems to have emerged from the EU's own internal evolution and can be seen, for example, in Europeans' approach to the international criminal court (pooling sovereignty) and their preference for hard targets in the Kyoto Protocol (analogous to the specific economic criteria of European Monetary Union). This approach finds a strong contrast in the longstanding American preference for flexibility and freedom of manoeuvre in international politics, a preference that is particularly strong in the current US administration. Moreover, if this American preference for freedom of action pushes it to pursue perpetual hegemony, a probable European reaction would be "Euro–Gaullism" — the pursuit of European unity for the sake of autonomy from the United States (Kühnhardt 2003, 12). While Kagan's argument is, by his own admission, a vast simplification, his ideas about Europe's self–perceived role in the world do identify a clear and substantive point of difference with the United States, and thus suggest a further reason why EU policy–makers are disinclined to pursue transatlantic interregionalism.

A realist analysis of international relations would lead us to expect the EU to maintain the preferences of the strong — i.e., like the United States, freedom of manoeuvre to pursue its interests and security. However, closer attention to how the EU externalises an approach to governance developed through its internal experience of building unity may be a better guide to understanding how EU and US perceptions of their interests and identities may continue to diverge; and if divergence is the order of the day, then the EU's disinclination to pursue an interregional commercial strategy toward a US–dominated North America is hardly surprising.

4. Conclusion

The commercial ties the European Union has developed with the countries of North America are strong, and will remain so for the foreseeable future.

While these relationships have developed separately, today they form a fairly coherent whole: EU trade with Canada, Mexico and the United States is mostly free and unproblematic, much like trade among the NAFTA members themselves. So why are EU policy–makers not seeking to formalise an inter-regional relationship with NAFTA in an often – discussed transatlantic free trade agreement (TAFTA)?

To some extent, the absence of transatlantic interregionalism can be explained in functionalist terms: there is no compelling economic rationale for a TAFTA, or for any overarching framework to codify transatlantic economic integration. Why fix what, despite some occasional sputterings, is not broken? But a functionalist approach ignores the politics behind Euro-pean trade strategies, a limitation this study has attempted to redress by considering three more politics–centred analytical lenses. However, it is diffi-cult to identify which of the three is most convincing in its explanation for the absence of an interregional strategy toward North America; none would predict such a strategy.

The interest group lens shows us why business groups have not promoted EU interregionalism toward North America with more vigour. The main reason lies in the moderate size of the potential gain. The status quo, though not ideal, is more or less acceptable for both advocates and opponents of liberalisation, while a TAFTA might not bring a large return for the former on their investment in mobilisation. Even though European officials have in the TABD and CERT sought to privilege and amplify the voices of pro–liberalisation groups (i.e., to reduce their costs of mobilisa-tion) these groups have not generated political momentum for an interre-gional strategy. The reason for their failure to do so cannot be found in the dissent of anti–liberalisation groups, which are much more concerned about the possible adjustments necessary in agreements with less developed countries. In already accessible markets such as those of North America, European business groups advocate technical, sector–specific agreements such as the Mutual Recognition Agreements and have little incentive to lobby EU policy–makers to initiate a significantly broader project like TAFTA. This contrasts sharply with many other cases of EU interregional-ism, in which the potential for broad and deep market opening exists, and thus business groups in particular have stronger incentives to mobilise for liberalising agreements.

Greater attention to international power dynamics brings into focus a big part of what is truly unique about transatlantic relations. Europe's commer-cial relationship with NAFTA cannot be understood outside the context of EU–US relations more generally. As the two main centres of established economic power in the world, each has a strategic incentive to secure export markets for its producers. The United States, whether in its creation of NAFTA, APEC, or an FTAA, presents a challenge to Europe's commercial position in the world. In this context, access to potentially lucrative markets is relative and, as its rationale for pursuing an FTA with Mexico (among others) suggests, the EU is very much concerned with its position relative to the United States. International trade and investment are the primary means through which economic power, influence and prosperity are redistributed across nations, and by which 'national' champions are created. Moreover, given the EU's difficulties in operationalising a common foreign and security policy — and the increasing gap between EU and US military capabilities — external commercial policy is the realistic locus of Europe's pursuit of relative material gain. Through this lens, a particularly clear picture of the limited prospects of an interregional strategy can be discerned.

While it is difficult to draw direct lines from questions of identities and culture to those of economic relationships, given the cultural content of trade and lingering questions about the coherence of the West, it is also useful to view EU commercial policy through the lens of identity considerations. Surely a shared sense of identity is not a sufficient condition for pursuing an interregional commercial relationship, nor is its absence sufficient to destroy interregionalism's prospects. Yet the EU's struggle to define its internal and external identities, and the omnipresence of an American superpower that insists on going its own way in international affairs, clearly provide a powerful incentive for the EU to define itself in contrast to the bullying hegemon — and a disincentive to tie itself more closely to it. While such a proposition is difficult to substantiate, and may be contingent on the parties and individuals in power in Washington and European capitals at any given time, it cannot be ignored in the current transatlantic political climate.

So, what does the EU–North American case tells us about EU interregional strategies in general? The initial reaction is one of scepticism: if the EU lacks a compelling reason to pursue an interregional strategy toward a region in which Europe has vital interests and which already has its own regional institution, how viable could interregionalism really be as a more general strategy? However, unlike other cases of EU interregionalism, this is the one in which the status quo terms of political and economic relations are acceptable from most relevant perspectives. A major impetus for transatlantic interregionalism would come only from a transformative event that created a new political rationale for such a strategy. In the absence of such an event, there seems little impetus for an interregional strategy — whether from interest groups, power politics or cultural/identity considerations; and given that major terrorist attacks in the United States, Spain and the United Kingdom have not been was not sufficiently transformative to create this new political rationale, it is probably best to hope that no truly transformative event does occur.

Thus, the absence of an EU interregional strategy toward North America does not necessarily undermine the conceptual or policy significance of interregionalism more generally. It does suggest that EU interregionalism is, at least at this point, primarily a strategy aimed at achieving gains the EU has been unable to reap through more traditional multilateral and bilateral channels. While there may not be a single, unified logic for pursuing an interregionalism, and while bilateral or multilateral approaches may serve specific goals more efficiently, interregionalism has generally proven productive — or at least not counterproductive — for almost all actors with an interest in EU foreign economic policy. The absence of an EU interregional strategy toward North America, in which the net gains from interregionalism would be far smaller than toward other regions, does not undermine this basic calculus; and if the current Doha Round of WTO negotiations were to falter, the appeal of an interregional strategy toward all regions, perhaps including North America, would grow.

Notes

1. In the authors' earlier work, interregionalism was analysed both as a policy strategy and a type of relationship. See Aggarwal & Fogarty (2004), pp. 4–6.
2. Notably, these lenses involve political, rather than economic, factors. Although there may be a market logic to these strategies, we start from the assumption that political factors drive policy-makers' choice of interregionalism as opposed to multilateralism, bilateralism and other trade strategies. See Grossman & Helpman (1996) regarding the economic rationality of interregionalism.
3. This section draws on Fogarty (2004).
4. In NTA negotiations, the US administration specifically requested the exclusion of Canadian business leaders from the TABD.
5. Canada seeks deal with EU, *The Gazette*, 17 April 2001.
6. In some circles in the United Kingdom, however, the welcome idea of closer ties with a North American community has converged with anti–EU sentiments to generate a different angle on Canadian ideas of closer partnership. A warm reception has been given to a few powerful North American voices (notably Conrad Black, the Canadian–born owner of the London *Daily Telegraph*, and former US senator Phil Gramm) calling for the United Kingdom to leave the European Union and join NAFTA. While this heterodox view has never made it into the mainstream of political discourse in the United Kingdom, yet EU Trade Commissioner Pascal Lamy felt it necessary in a mid–2000 speech to acknowledge and then to criticise this viewpoint (Lamy 2000).
7. In terms of the guest editors' definition of types of regionalism in the Introduction to this collection, NAFTA represents 'first–generation regionalism' — a hegemon–inspired agreement whose dominant focus is economic (trade and investment).
8. One open question here is, of course, whether NAFTA would itself 'disappear' as a separate entity within an FTAA, or whether it would continue to exist as a nested arrangement under the FTAA. This question will probably remain open until FTAA negotiations progress further.
9. The EU's overt promotion of 'counterpart coherence' in its policies toward Mercosur, the Southern Mediterranean, and East Asia suggests its policy–makers have this sort of regionalist diffusion very much in mind. On the concept of counterpart coherence, see Aggarwal & Fogarty (2004), pp. 17–19.
10. For a discussion of interest group politics in the EU, see Greenwood (1997) and Dupont (2001).
11. While we discuss interest groups here in terms of sectors, others have analysed social and economic group preferences in terms of factors — i.e., land, labour and capital. See Rogowski (1989), Frieden (1991), Frieden & Rogowski (1996), and Hiscox (2001) for discussions of when economic actors split along sectoral and factoral lines.
12. Because North American standards tend to be similar to European ones, European labour, environmental, and other societal groups interested in international trade generally do not engage in the level of advocacy in the EU's commercial policy toward North America as they do *vis–à–vis* other, less–developed regions. As such, we focus our analysis here on European commercial sectors.
13. 'Thrashing around', *The Economist*, 1 June 2002.
14. The *New York Times* identified US–EU disagreements on this issue as based in fundamental philosophical differences regarding the 'precautionary principle' — i.e., whether GMOs (genetically modified organisms) must be scientifically proven 'innocent' before they may be imported or proven 'guilty' before their import could be banned. The United States takes the latter position, the EU the former. *The New York Times*, 25 May 2003.
15. On the relative merits of sectoral and more broad–based commercial agreements, see Aggarwal & Ravenhill (2001).
16. See Bhagwati & Arvind (1996) and Sapir (1998) regarding this 'hub–and–spoke' model of EU–centred commercial agreements.

17. The EU's overt rationale for concluding a free trade agreement with Mexico in 1999 was to redress the 'NAFTA effect', specifically the Europeans' worsened terms of trade with Mexico. In a document reporting the conclusion of negotiations with Mexico (European Commission 2000), the Commission repeatedly couches the benefits of the agreement in terms of its value as a response to NAFTA. See Faust (2004) for more on the EU–Mercosur relationship.

18. Of course, other factors contributed to the lack of recent progress in APEC and ASEM, notably the disruption of the 1998 Asian economic crisis and the restarting of multilateral trade negotiations after 1999. See Gilson (2004) for a comprehensive discussion of ASEM. Regarding APEC, see Aggarwal & Morrison (1998).

19. Manners (2001) has suggested that European leaders have sought to foster an overall European identity through comparison to other peer nations. More generally, Karl Deutsch and his colleagues have argued that commercial interactions can generate feelings of mutual identification (Deutsch *et al.* 1957; Deutsch 1966).

20. The cultural element of the purported 'Old v. New Europe' distinction may be overdrawn. In a 2003 Pew Research poll, different Europeans were asked whether they thought that "when differences occur with America, it is because of [my country's] different values." Some 33 per cent of French and 37 per cent of German respondents answered "yes", compared to 62 per cent of Czechs. Cited in Judt (2003).

21. For instance, as Lawrence Wright argued in the *New Yorker*, elements of Al–Qaeda targeted Madrid in March 2004 not to punish Spain for its participation in the US–led coalition in Iraq, but because it represents Christendom's eclipse of Islam in the late Middle Ages. See L. Wright, 'The Terror Web,' *New Yorker*, 2 August 2004.

22. Some have cast Europe as a 'civilian power', which highlights the normative aspects of Europe's values and identity (i.e., democracy, the rule of law, economic justice, pooling of sovereignty, etc.) and implicitly or explicitly juxtaposes them to other leading nations (especially the military, commercial and technological 'hyperpower' of the United States). For two distinct approaches to this idea, see Prodi (2000) and Kagan (2003). Inglehart (1988) has similarly characterised Europe as representing a 'postmodern' society, increasingly postmaterialist and environmentalist in nature, while the United States represents a hypermodern society, consumerist to its core.

23. Waever (1998) has suggested that a convergence of European and American identities necessarily undermines the goal of creating a European identity.

24. Henry Kissinger, in a July 2001 interview on National Public Radio, accused European policy–makers of stirring up anti–American sentiment to bolster European solidarity. Pascal Lamy similarly observed that the best way to get a rousing ovation in the European Parliament these days is to denounce the United States. The *Economist*, 7 July 2001.

25. Manners (2002), pp. 240–241 has located the source of Europe's "normative power" and international identity in three factors: (1) the historical context of the post–war need to overcome nationalism; (2) the "hybrid polity" of supranational and intergovernmental institutions that "transcends Westphalian norms"; and (3) Europe's "political–legal constitution," which enshrines the norms of democracy, human rights and social justice.

References

Aggarwal, V. & Fogarty, E. (2004) Between Regionalism and Globalism: European Union Interregional Trade Strategies, in: V. Aggarwal & E. Fogarty (eds) *EU Trade Strategies: Between Regionalism and Globalism* (New York: Palgrave).

Aggarwal, V. & Morrison, C. (eds) (1998) *Asia–Pacific Crossroads: Regime Creation and the Future of APEC* (New York: St. Martin's Press).

Aggarwal, V. & Ravenhill, J. (2001) How open sectoral agreements undermine the WTO, *Asia–Pacific Issues* 50.

Bhagwati, J. N. & Arvind, P. (1996) Preferential trading areas and multilateralism: strangers, friends, or foes?, in: J. N. Bhagwati & A. Panagariya (eds) *Free Trade Areas or Free Trade? The Economics of Preferential Trade Agreements* (Washington, DC: AEI Press).

Blair, T. (2001) Speech to Canadian Parliament (Ottawa, 23 February).

Council of Europe (2000) Prospects for a new transatlantic trade relationship, Report of the Committee on Economic Affairs and Development to the Parliamentary Assembly, 6 June.

Department of Trade and Industry, United Kingdom (DTI) (2001) World trade and international trade rules: North America, available at: http://www.dti.gov.uk/worldtrade/namerica.htm (accessed [date])

Deutsch, K. *et al.* (1957) *Political Community: North–Atlantic Area* (New York: Greenwood Press).

Deutsch, K. (1966) *Nationalism and Social Communication: An Inquiry into the Foundations of Nationality* (Cambridge: MIT Press).

Dupont, C. (2001) Euro–pressure: avenues and strategies for lobbying the European Union, in: V. Aggarwal (ed.) *Winning in Asia, European Style: Market and Nonmarket Strategies for Success* (New York: Palgrave).

European Commission (2003) EU–US bilateral economic relations. Available at: www.europa.eu.int/comm/external_relations/US/sum06_04/econ.pdf (accessed July 2005).

European Commission, DG Trade (2000) Communication from the Commission to the Council and the European Parliament accompanying the final text of the draft decisions by the EC–Mexico Joint Council, Brussels, 18 January.

Faust, J. (2004) Blueprint for an Interregional Future? The European Union and the Southern Cone, in: V. Aggarwal & E. Fogarty (eds) *EU Trade Strategies: Between Regionalism and Globalism* (New York: Palgrave).

Fogarty, E. (2004) Be Careful What You Wish For: European Union and North America, in: V. Aggarwal & E. Fogarty (eds) *EU Trade Strategies: Between Regionalism and Globalism* (New York: Palgrave).

Fogarty, E. (2005) The dog that barked (did it bite?): the antiglobalisation movement and the multilateral trade regime, paper presented at the 'Annual Conference of the International Studies Association', Honolulu, 13 March.

Frieden, J. (1991) Invested interests: the politics of national economic policies in a world of global finance, *International Organization* 45(4), pp. 425–451.

Frieden, J. & Rogowski, R. (1996) The impact of the international economy on national policies: an analytical overview, in: R. Keohane & H. Milner (eds) *Internationalization and Domestic Politics* (Cambridge: Cambridge University Press).

Gilson, J. (2004) Weaving a New Silk Road: Europe Meets Asia, in: V. Aggarwal & E. Fogarty (eds) *EU Trade Strategies: Between Regionalism and Globalism* (New York: Palgrave).

Gower, M. (2000) Titans of trade: signing free–trade deals with heavyweights like North America and the European Union has placed Mexico on the world stage, American Chamber of Commerce of Mexico, 1 October.

Greenwood, J. (1997) *Representing Interests in the European Union* (New York: St. Martin's Press).

Grossman, G. & E. Helpman (1996) Electoral competition and special interest politics, *Review of Economic Studies* 63, pp. 265–286.

Hiscox, M. (2001) Class versus industry cleavages: inter–industry factor mobility and the politics of trade, *International Organization* 55(1), pp. 1–46.

Inglehart, R. (1988) The Renaissance of political culture, *American Political Science Review* 82(4), pp. 1120–1130.

Judt, T. (2003) Old Europe, New Europe — US illusions, book review on Countercurrents.org, 8 March.

Kagan, R. (2003) *Of Paradise and Power: America and Europe in the New World Order* (New York: Knopf).

Kühnhardt, L. (2003) Contrasting Transatlantic Interpretations: The EU and the US Towards a Common Global Role, *Occasional Paper 2003:1* (Stockholm: SIEPS).

Lamy, P. (1999) Speech to Transatlantic Business Dialogue (Brussels, 23 May).

Lamy, P. (2000) Speech to Confederation of British Industry (London, 6 July).

Manners, I. (2002) Normative power Europe: a contradiction in terms?, *Journal of Common Market Studies* 40(2), pp. 235–258.

Manners, I. (2001) The 'difference engine': constructing and representing the international identity in the European Union, Web paper downloaded from CIAOnet.

Prodi, R. (2000) *Europe As I See It* (Cambridge: Polity).

Rogowski, R. (1989) *Commerce and Coalitions: How Trade Affects Domestic Political Alignments* (Princeton: Princeton University Press).

Sapir, A. (1998) The political economy of EC regionalism, *European Economic Review* 42, pp. 717–732.

Sbragia, A. (2001) European Union and NAFTA, in: M. Telò (ed.) *European Union and New Regionalism: Regional Actors and Global Governance in a Post–Hegemonic Era* (London: Ashgate).

Wæver, O. (1998) Integration as security: constructing a Europe at peace, in: C. Kupchan (ed.) *Atlantic Security* (New York: Council on Foreign Relations).

The EU and Central and Eastern Europe: The Absence of Interregionalism

KAREN E. SMITH

1. Introduction

The European Union's relations with Central and Eastern Europe are not an example of 'interregionalism', or bloc–to–bloc relations. Rather, regionalism in Europe is encouraged through enlargement of the EU itself, which has in turn inhibited the development of 'sub–regionalism' in Central and Eastern Europe. This study analyses why this is the case, by exploring the tensions between 'bilateralism' and interregionalism in the EU's relations with the Central and East European countries (CEECs). Since the end of the Cold War, the EU has developed intensive bilateral relations with each of its neighbours, which allows it to apply economic and political conditionality — that is, use leverage — and thus differentiate between fast and slow reformers. Bilateralism and differentiation were particularly apparent during the enlargement process. The EU has also tried to encourage its neighbours to cooperate with each other, but it never insisted on regional cooperation and strong sub–regional groupings have not evolved in Central and Eastern Europe. The implications of this approach to regionalism in Europe are far–reaching, notably in southeastern Europe where the tensions between the development of bilateral relations (intended to lead to the accession of those countries that meet the EU's membership conditions) and sub–regional cooperation are most evident. But it also poses challenges for the EU in its relations with former Soviet republics — and even with the southern Mediterranean countries as well.

The next section defines the important terms used in this study. The third notes the importance of regional cooperation as an objective of the EU's foreign relations, to highlight the extent to which relations with Central and Eastern Europe have not followed the norm. In the fourth section, the tensions between bilateralism and interregionalism in the EU's relations with Central and Eastern Europe are analysed. The concluding section notes the implications of the EU's policy in Central and Eastern Europe for its relations with other areas of Europe.

2. Definitions

'Regionalism' here denotes institutionalised cooperation (which may or may not be in the form of a formal regional organisation) among countries within geographical proximity of each other. Shared interests and/or shared values and identities can prompt countries to cooperate with each other (region–building from within); outsiders can also try to foster regionalism (region–building from outside). 'Sub–regionalism' indicates the development of sub–regional institutionalised cooperation, here specifically among fewer European countries than the total number of members of the European Union or the other major European organisations, which by now are, or are nearly, continental in scope (NATO, the Organisation for Security and Cooperation in Europe, the Council of Europe). Again, sub–regionalism can arise from within and/or be encouraged by outsiders.

'Interregionalism' refers to the relationships between regional (and/or sub–regional) groupings. It can also be a policy goal of one or more of those groupings, or states within those groupings. 'Bilateralism' here indicates the relationship between the EU (as a unit) on the one hand, and an individual third country (not a grouping of third countries) on the other. The EU is thus conceptualised as an actor, able to function actively and deliberately in relation to other actors in the international system (see Sjöstedt 1977, 15). In fact, there is a quite a developed system in place that has been designed to enable the EU to do just that. And on occasion — certainly not all of the time — the member states and EU institutions can recognise shared interests, agree objectives, and formulate and implement common policies to pursue them.[1] The EU can thus be seen as one actor engaging in relations with other actors; those relations are bilateral when the other actors are individual countries. They are interregional when the other actors are regional or sub–regional groupings.

3. Regional Cooperation as an EU Foreign Policy Objective

Soon after its formation, the European Community[2] was advocating regional cooperation and the creation of regional organisations around the world, and continued to do so throughout the period of the Cold War. The end of the Cold War sparked a new wave of regionalism (Fawcett 1995), further increasing the Union's activity in support of regional cooperation, and vindicating the regional approach. The EU deals with countries prima–rily on a regional basis, a striking and unusual feature of its foreign relations; no other international actor does this to the same extent. Of course, it has important relationships with individual countries but, by and large, the EU's relations with third countries are grouped according to regions. It prefers to deal with third countries collectively: it lays out regional strategies, sets up aid programmes on a regional basis, and concludes specific kinds of agreements with countries in a particular region. The EU then strongly encourages the countries grouped regionally to cooperate with each other. Most EU aid programmes now allocate around 10 per cent of total aid to regional cooperation.

Where regional groupings (whether formal organisations or looser frame–works for cooperation) have formed, or where countries are considering forming a regional grouping, the Union usually supports them actively. The EU has concluded cooperation agreements with several regional groupings. According to the Commission, these agreements contribute to "the reinforce–ment of regional identity and of the regional institutions" (European Commission 1995b, 18). This is particularly the case where the bloc–to–bloc cooperation agreement is the only formal link with the members of the regional grouping (the African, Caribbean and Pacific countries; the Andean Community; the Association of South–East Asian Nations; the Central American community; and the Gulf Cooperation Council).

The EU conducts regular political dialogues with an even larger number of regional groupings, not all of which are as integrated as the organisations just mentioned. The dialogues allow for discussion of issues of mutual interest — they are not primarily about discussing the state of regional cooperation. But they encourage cooperation in that they spur the regional grouping to collab–orate and cooperate before, during, and after meetings: "The central elements of the *acquis politique* of the EU encourage regional cooperation and peaceful regional conflict resolution. Group–to–group dialogues are obviously the most appropriate means to encourage such developments and to influence regional groupings in this direction, if necessary with the help of various economic and financial incentives of the Community" (Monar 1997, 269–270).

The Union's strong support for regional cooperation stems from the belief, born of its own experience, that it provides the basis for peace, economic development and prosperity. However, the EU has other interests in fostering regional cooperation, including facilitating trade and investment by EU economic actors; and there are obvious economies of scale in dealing with regional groupings rather than separate countries. The EU's promotion of regional cooperation is also clearly one area where the EU stands out, internationally. In a world of apparently increasing regionalism, the EU is superbly well placed to shape and encourage the trend, and to exercise leadership.

4. The Exceptionalism of Central and Eastern Europe

Central and Eastern Europe, however, has always been an exception to this general rule of EU support for regional cooperation. Already during the Cold War, the Council for Mutual Economic Assistance (CMEA), the organisation for 'economic cooperation' among communist countries, was a high–profile exception to the Community's support for regional groupings. Through the early 1980s, the CMEA sought bloc–to–bloc relations with the Community, but the Community viewed it as an instrument of Soviet domination over Eastern Europe, and insisted on developing relations with the CMEA member countries separately. The ensuing stalemate was broken only after Mikhail Gorbachev assumed power in the Soviet Union and agreed to the Community's demands.

In June 1988, the Community and the CMEA established official relations, which paved the way for bilateral relations between the Community and CMEA member countries. Bilateralism allowed the Community to differentiate among the Central and East European countries: those countries that were further ahead in the reform process were accorded more beneficial treatment. Conditionality was used to encourage political and economic reforms, which the Community considered crucial for ensuring European security: free–trading, democratic countries make better neighbours because they do not pose a threat to security. Conditionality cannot be applied without differentiation and therefore both depends on and reproduces bilateralism.

Following the EC–CMEA declaration, trade and cooperation agreements were negotiated with CMEA countries that were implementing reforms. They were concluded first with Hungary (1988), then Poland (1989), Czechoslovakia (1990), Bulgaria (1990) and Romania (1991) — as each proved they were implementing reforms. In addition, starting in the second half of 1989, the Community granted aid through the PHARE programme.[3] Again, aid was extended on a conditional (and therefore bilateral and differentiated) basis, first to Poland and Hungary, then to other countries.

The cooperation agreements and aid were not enough to meet the expectations of the CEECs, almost all of whom immediately declared that their number one foreign policy priority was to join the European Community (soon to be Union). The Community's initial response, however, was to stall:

instead of membership negotiations, it offered the Central and East European countries special association ('Europe') agreements, again on a bilateral and conditional basis. Only countries that were clearly committed to the rule of law, respect for human rights, the establishment of a multi–party system, free and fair elections and the introduction of market economies were eligible. The first to make the grade were Czechoslovakia, Hungary and Poland in 1991; then Bulgaria and Romania in 1993; and then the three Baltic republics and Slovenia in 1995 and 1996.[4]

The Union's approach to Central and Eastern Europe was not wholly a bilateral one, however, in the sense that the cooperation and Europe agreements were tailored for each CEEC, but were similar in terms of conditionality and key provisions (such as political dialogue). Likewise, the PHARE programme was a regional one, designed specifically for the CEECs. But the agreements were still bilateral, and the benefits available under PHARE still conditional on how a particular country was performing. Some observers warned that this 'hub–and–spoke' bilateralism could damage economic growth, as the CEECs reoriented their trade to the EU but kept up barriers between themselves.[5]

The EU and the CEECs, however, had effectively closed off alternatives. The Community did originally offer to conclude a single Europe agreement with Czechoslovakia, Hungary and Poland, but they refused.[6] PHARE aid was also used to foster regional cooperation, and PHARE multi–country programmes have existed since 1991. The creation of the Visegrad group — between Czechoslovakia, Hungary and Poland — in February 1991 was welcomed by the Community;[7] in fact, the Union pushed the Visegrad group to form a free trade area, which it did by creating the Central European Free Trade Agreement in 1992. Also in 1992, the Community launched dialogues with the Visegrad group and the three Baltic republics, specifically to encourage the sub–regional groupings. External Relations Commissioner Frans Andriessen commented in 1992 that: "Already a process has begun between the Community and the three Visegrad countries which points towards a multilateralisation of relations between the parties involved. This could provide a valuable model for other countries in the future" (Andriessen 1992).

In 1993, the dialogues developed into a structured relationship which entailed regular meetings of all the associates and various formations of the Council, in all policy areas of the EU. The Commission claimed this "strengthens intra–regional cooperation among the CEEC's [sic] themselves when dealing with the Institutions of the Union" (European Commission 1995a, 1). But the CEECs preferred the bilateral approach, and in 1997, the structured relationship was dismantled, although it continued on foreign policy issues.

The CEECs, then, did not enthusiastically embrace the EU's rather limited policy favouring regional cooperation; in fact, they viewed it suspiciously. Some CEECs claimed that the encouragement of regional cooperation was an attempt to block their accession to the EU because a separate regional grouping could serve as an alternative to EU membership (Körmendy 1992,

248; Adamiec 1993, 24–25); and they did not want to recreate the CMEA, or encourage the Union to postpone consideration of enlargement.

In response, the EU never forced the CEECs to cooperate with each other, and bilateralism predominated. There was in fact a strong current of opinion within the Union that enlargement was an historical necessity, which could at most be postponed but could not be denied. The Union (including even the most reluctant member states) never seriously considered *never* enlarging. The path was thus clearly towards enlargement, not towards the development of bloc–to–bloc relations between the two sides of the former Iron Curtain. Of course, the CEECs were not happy about the pace of the enlargement process, but they had still successfully convinced the EU member states that enlargement — and therefore bilateralism — was the only viable policy option.

In June 1993, the Copenhagen European Council finally agreed that enlargement to the Central and East European countries could take place, but it again set conditions. Applicant countries were to have achieved a functioning market economy; democracy, the rule of law, and protection of human rights and minorities; and the ability to assume the obligations of EU membership, the *acquis communautaire* (European Council 1993, 13). The Copenhagen conditions were specified for those countries that had concluded (or were in the process of negotiating) Europe agreements, which at the time meant six countries: Bulgaria, the Czech Republic, Hungary, Poland, Romania and Slovakia. The prospect of enlargement was thus still relatively contained and manageable, but could not remain so. Four newly independent countries — Estonia, Latvia, Lithuania and Slovenia — could not reasonably be left out of the process and, in December 1994, the European Council affirmed that these four countries met the conditions for Europe agreements and would thus be formally included in the membership queue. All ten CEECs applied for membership between 1994 and 1996. In June 1994, the Corfu European Council also extended membership invitations to Malta and the Republic of Cyprus.

The prospect of membership and the consequent use of membership conditionality are the pre–eminent examples of bilateralism in the EU's relations with the CEECs. Each membership application was judged separately by the Commission, and the Council decided to open negotiations accordingly. In principle, such differentiation should spur progress with reforms in each individual applicant country and a healthy competition between the applicant countries to join first.

There were worries, however, that the application of membership conditionality — part, after all, of a strategy to spread peace and security — could actually end up destabilising applicant countries, as it isolates and excludes (for a time) some states. And it would certainly not constitute an incentive for the applicant countries to cooperate with each other. This was of particular concern where there were tensions or unresolved disputes between the applicant countries, or between the applicant countries and their non–EU neighbours. So the overwhelming importance of bilateralism and differentiation had to be softened. The EU tried to do this in three successive ways: by taking a more sub–regional approach to relations with the CEECs and their neighbours, by establishing an inclusive 'accession process', and by opening negotiations with all of them.

First, the EU tried to encourage more sub–regionalism. The concern about increased tensions or even conflicts among the CEECs made it imperative that these be resolved before enlargement, lest the Union import instability and insecurity, or generate tensions between an enlarged EU and outsiders. Across Central and Eastern Europe, there were inter–state disputes over minority rights and boundaries, and domestic tensions stemming from minorities' grievances, economic hardship and nationalism (this quite apart from the wars in the former Yugoslavia or former Soviet republics such as Moldova, Armenia and Azerbaijan, and Georgia). The most serious of these were between Hungary, Slovakia and Romania — largely over Hungarian minorities — and between the three Baltic republics and Russia — largely over Russian minorities.

The foremost attempt by the EU to encourage cooperation among the CEECs, and thus resolve such tensions and disputes, was the 1994/95 Pact for Stability. The EU (prompted particularly by France) sponsored this year–long conference, in which the ten CEECs were strongly encouraged to reach agreements among themselves on borders and the treatment of minorities, and to identify projects for regional cooperation which could be funded by the EU (Final Conference on the Pact on Stability in Europe 1995, 113). Largely through the Pact, the EU did succeed in cajoling Hungary and Romania, and Slovakia and Romania, to reach 'good–neighbour' agreements. The Pact later served as a precedent for a similar initiative in southeastern Europe (see section 5 below), and for the development of a soft 'good–neighbourliness' condition for EU membership. In Agenda 2000, the Commission stated that "before accession, applicants should make every effort to resolve any outstanding border dispute among themselves or involving third countries. Failing this they should agree that the dispute be referred to the International Court of Justice [ICJ]" (European Commission 1997a, 51). The Helsinki European Council reiterated this condition: applicants had to resolve outstanding border disputes before accession, or refer them to the ICJ.[8] This is not, it should be noted, a requirement to cooperate with each other in general, only to resolve disputes.

Through PHARE, the EU supported sub–regional cooperation. In 1994, the PHARE cross–border cooperation programme was initiated; this aided cooperation between border regions in PHARE countries and in EU member states, and tried to eliminate bottlenecks at border crossings between PHARE countries. The European Commission boasted that PHARE programmes "have proved extremely effective mechanisms for stimulating a dialogue among the CEECs, for harmonising policies between the CEECs, for linking national programmes in each of the countries to common regional strategies and for assuring a demand–driven approach to programme formulation" (European Commission 1995a, 3).

The EU also stepped up its support for European sub–regional groupings, such as the Visegrad group and Central European Free Trade Area (CEFTA),

Council of Baltic Sea States (CBSS), Barents Euro–Arctic Council (BEAC), Black Sea Economic Cooperation (BSEC) and Central European Initiative (CEI) (see Appendix for the membership of these organisations). Many of these groupings were the fruit of EU member state initiatives; the Visegrad group and BSEC (driven by Turkey) are notable exceptions. All are strictly intergovernmental, weakly institutionalised, not well resourced, and depend fully on the will of their members to make something of them (Bailes 1999, 158–159).

The June 1996 Florence European Council asked the Commission to promote regional cooperation among partner countries, notably those forming the CEI (European Council 1996; European Commission 1996b). Italy held the presidency, and had founded the CEI, so the European Council decision is unsurprising. Likewise, several member states (notably Finland and Sweden) pushed for links with the Council of Baltic Sea States in accordance with the 'Northern Dimension' initiative, which tries to strengthen links between the EU, Norway, the Baltic republics and Russia (European Commission 1996a). The Commission is a member of CBSS and BEAC, and participates in CEI meetings, and the EU has funded cooperation projects agreed within the Central European Initiative and the Baltic Sea Cooperation Council. Such financial support is crucial: the CEI's cooperation fund in 2002, for example, had an annual budget of only 300,000 euros, of which 81,000 came from Italy.[9]

Support for these sub–regional groupings was seen as a way to maintain links between an enlarging EU and those countries left out of the first (and successive) rounds of enlargement. The Commission views such schemes "as a way of bolstering stability between the countries concerned", thus minimising the possibilities that enlargement will spark tensions between the new insiders and outsiders (European Commission 1996b, 1; see also European Commission 1997b).

However, the EU's attempts to encourage sub–regionalism did not reduce the centrality of the bilateral and differentiated relationships between the EU and each CEEC, which were dominated by the accession process. The other two ways of lessening the impact of differentiation were, in practice, just ways of deferring it, because they dealt with the impact of exclusion from membership negotiations, not from membership itself. Both ways, in practice, kept as many countries together as possible — a sort of softer version of bilateralism.

The EU initially developed an inclusive 'accession process', launched at the same time as the decisions were made in 1997 to differentiate between two groups of applicant countries and to begin membership negotiations with only one of them. In its Agenda 2000 report in July 1997, the European Commission recommended that membership negotiations be opened with five CEECs: the Czech Republic, Estonia, Hungary, Poland and Slovenia (plus Cyprus) (European Commission 1997a). The decision to include Estonia and Slovenia, in addition to the three countries traditionally considered the frontrunners (the Czech Republic, Hungary and Poland) was influenced by NATO's June 1997 decision to expand to only three countries in the first instance, the Czech Republic, Hungary and Poland.[10] The EU's first round of enlargement would be larger, partly in the interests of stability.

In December 1997, the Luxembourg European Council agreed with the Commission's recommendation and, in March 1998, membership negotiations formally began with Cyprus, the Czech Republic, Estonia, Hungary, Poland and Slovenia. Accession Partnerships were drawn up for all the applicant countries, listing the objectives that the EU wanted each applicant to meet. The Commission reported annually on progress made. The accession process kept up the pressure on all the applicants, since only those countries that met the membership conditions would join, while the remaining applicant countries were promised that, if they made good progress towards meeting them, then they too could start accession talks. Differentiation thus continued to dominate the enlargement process.

However, the EU's strategy started to unravel within a year, paradoxically because it worked quite quickly. Latvia and Lithuania made rapid progress in meeting the conditions, and elections in Slovakia in September 1998 produced a reformist government. Thus, by late 1998, three more CEECs (plus Malta) were close to joining those already negotiating accession, leaving Bulgaria and Romania in the 'slow lane'. Excluding Bulgaria and Romania became untenable, however, when the Kosovo war erupted in March 1999. UK Prime Minister Tony Blair, in particular, pressed this point. The risks of further isolating Bulgaria and Romania — given the instability in their neighbourhood and the support they had given to NATO action — made it unfeasible to leave them out of the next round of negotiations.

In October 1999, the Commission recommended that the EU open negotiations with *all* of the applicant countries: this would make a "decisive contribution to stability and prosperity" in Europe, a political imperative for the EU.[11] The Helsinki European Council in December 1999 agreed to open negotiations with the six countries, because it was "determined to lend a positive contribution to security and stability on the European continent" (European Council 1999, para 10). The EU would still complete talks with each country only as it was ready — again, differentiation was to guide the accession process, but there was a clear trend towards grouping the applicant countries together. However, the EU was only deferring the basic dilemma: at some point, countries would inevitably be excluded from the first round of eastern enlargement, whatever the political implications.

Debate then turned to how many countries would join in that first round, and it soon became apparent that there was much reluctance to exclude countries from it. In 2000, support for a 'big–bang' enlargement — up to ten candidate countries joining at once — grew among observers, though not yet among all the member states. Taking in ten countries together would leave fewer on the outside, minimising the difficulties caused by differentiation and bilateralism. The Commission eventually joined the big–bang bandwagon: in early September 2001, Enlargement Commissioner Gunter Verheugen maintained that ten countries could join in the next round of enlargement: all of the candidates except for Bulgaria and Romania (Verheugen 2001).

The terrorist attacks on the US then reinforced the security rationale for the big–bang option. In November 2001, the Commission declared that "[a] strong and united Europe is more important than ever before, against the background of the terrorist attacks of 11 September and subsequent developments", and stated that ten candidate countries could conclude negotiations by the end of 2002 (European Commission 2001a, 4). And so it was: after final intensive negotiations, the December 2002 Copenhagen European Council accepted that ten countries would accede to the EU on 1 May 2004. As for Bulgaria and Romania, the Copenhagen European Council stated that the objective was to welcome them as members in 2007.[12]

Thus, the dilemmas posed by bilateralism and differentiation with respect to the CEECs were overcome by relaxing conditionality (and therefore bilateralism), to an extent, in favour of a more inclusive approach. This has worked, in that the big–bang enlargement of the EU was a colossal expansion of its regionalist model across the old Iron Curtain. Interregionalism did not figure much at all in the enlargement process: although ten countries joined the EU at the same time, they did not form a cohesive grouping; all were negotiating separately. In fact, attempts by some Visegrad countries to coordinate negotiating strategies on the financial aspects failed because Poland, in particular, sought the best possible deal for itself — though all the candidate countries fought for themselves, and the EU most certainly did not encourage them to cooperate during the negotiations.[13] Some observers have cautioned that the way the EU expanded regionalism across Central and Eastern Europe has drawbacks. For Pál Dunay, by failing to contribute to interregionalism — an "obvious shortcoming of EU policy" — the EU has not been encouraging the mutual identification that will ease the new member states' integration into the EU — a failure which has implications for the functioning of the enlarged EU (Dunay 2004, 40).

The enlargement process also has implications, firstly, for sub–regionalism and, secondly, as discussed in section 5, for the rest of Europe. Sub–regional groups that consist entirely of new EU member states (such as the Visegrad group) could simply disappear altogether.[14] As a condition of membership, the new member states had to leave CEFTA, for example, and, once Bulgaria and Romania join the EU, CEFTA will disappear.[15] Of course, neighbouring countries within the EU do cooperate with each other (for the obvious reasons that prompt neighbours to do so), and there are numerous programmes funded by the Commission to encourage precisely that, but permanent coalitions are rare in the EU: the Benelux or the Franco–German couple do not hold together under all conditions, for example. Politics within the EU demands that states be flexible enough to seek out different coalitions for different purposes.

The sub–regional groupings that link together current EU member states, future member states and outsiders could also be fatally strained as a result of enlargement, although admittedly some could usefully serve as 'bridges' between the enlarged EU and outsiders — notably Russia. But if the aim of outsiders is to join the EU, they have little incentive to devote much attention to sub–regional groupings, whose resources are, in any event, limited. Even if EU membership is not on the cards, the economic and even political dominance of the EU dictates that outsiders revolve around it to some extent; cooperation within sub–regional organisations may be a way 'inside', but will remain of secondary importance. However, as Andrew Cottey points out, where sub-regions are defined in significant part by geography — and therefore interdependence — states have concrete interests and problems that can be best addressed by sub–regional groupings. One such sub–region is that surrounding the Black Sea; another is that around the Baltic Sea (Cottey 1999, 247). But the future of 'bridging' sub–regional organisations also depends on EU member states, and particularly the new ones, devoting attention to the sub–regional groupings, something which is difficult to juggle given the exigencies of participating in EU programmes, the Common Foreign and Security Policy, and the Area of Freedom, Security and Justice.[16]

5. Implications for the Rest of Europe

The enlargement issue now hangs over all attempts by the EU to promote sub–regional cooperation elsewhere in Europe. The Treaty of European Union makes it clear that any European state that respects the principles of liberty, democracy, respect for human rights and fundamental freedoms, and the rule of law, can apply to join the Union.[17] Applicants would have to meet the Copenhagen criteria to join but, in principle, the EU is otherwise open to any European state; and even though ten states have just joined in 2004, two more are about to join in 2007, and Turkey is waiting in the wings, there are still many more potential candidates. This, to put it mildly, complicates the EU's attempts to encourage those potential candidates to cooperate with each other: the path to accession is one taken by individual countries, not groups of them.

As in Central and Eastern Europe, the EU's relations with other European countries are based on regional strategies. It deals with two groups of states, the southeast European countries and the East European countries (all formerly part of the Soviet Union). There is a 'template' agreement for relations between individual countries of each group and the EU (Stabilisation and Association agreements; Partnership and Cooperation agreements), and aid is provided under framework programmes (CARDS; TACIS). The EU has also — to a much greater extent in southeastern Europe than elsewhere — tried to induce the countries in each group to cooperate with each other, and funding is devoted specifically for that purpose. At the same time, it has explicitly promised EU membership to southeast European countries, but not to the East European countries.

By far the EU's most active and coercive promotion of sub–regional cooperation has been in southeastern Europe since 1995. In December 1995, following the Dayton peace agreement, the EU launched the Royaumont Process, which was to encourage the normalization of relations between the countries concerned (Albania, Bosnia–Herzegovina, Croatia, the Former Yugoslav Republic of Macedonia or FYROM, and the Federal Republic of Yugoslavia). The EU also devised a 'regional approach'. In April 1997, the

General Affairs Council set political and economic conditions for trade relations, provision of assistance and contractual relations with the five southeast European countries, which included a readiness to engage in cross–border cooperation (Council of the EU 1997, 132–134). A special aid programme for reconstruction and rehabilitation was set up (originally OBNOVA, then renamed CARDS); it also funds regional cooperation and good–neighbourliness programmes.

The EU's strategy was revised during the 1999 Kosovo war. The Royamount Process was replaced by the Stability Pact for southeastern Europe. New Stabilisation and Association Agreements (SAAs) are on offer, but with strict conditionality attached. The SAA process effectively strengthens bilateral links between the EU and each country, although both the Stability Pact and the SAAs state that regional cooperation is necessary to solve the problems of the region. As the Finnish Presidency and Commission noted in December 1999, the "Stability Pact reflects the widespread recognition that regional problems require regional solutions" (Finnish Presidency and European Commission 1999).

This regionalist strategy, however, is overshadowed by the EU enlargement process. The prospect of eventual EU accession was held out for southeast European countries in the Stability Pact initiative, because it is considered to be the most powerful policy instrument the EU has to encourage the countries to participate in the initiative and to undertake desired reforms (Council of the EU 1999). They would have to meet the membership conditions, but they were given a definite promise that, if they did so, the EU would enlarge to include them. In response, Croatia applied for EU membership in February 2003; FYROM did so in March 2004.

The promise of membership was made to encourage reforms to help ensure security in the region, but it means that the countries will be judged and rewarded separately, i.e., that each is on its own path to membership. Enlargement still entails differentiation — difficult to reconcile with the demand that southeast European countries cooperate with each other. And in southeastern Europe, there are very large differences among the countries: some are lagging far behind and so would join the EU much later than any frontrunners. The option of a 'big–bang' southeast European enlargement is simply not feasible, unless the EU tells the frontrunners to wait; and the EU has patently decided not to do so. In June 2004, the European Council agreed with a largely positive Commission opinion on Croatia's application, and stated that membership negotiations could open with that country in 2005.

Yet politics in the region are still tinged with extreme nationalism, and minority rights issues remain volatile. In this atmosphere, bilateralism and differentiation may not produce the benign competition we saw in Central and Eastern Europe. The promise of eventual enlargement, made in a clear attempt to encourage southeastern Europe to embark on a post–national 'European' path, could have consequences that the EU has difficulty managing.

With respect to the remaining potential membership candidates from Europe, the EU has been trying to delay even offering a prospect of membership until far into the future, but has not been active in encouraging regional cooperation instead. In early 1992, the EU decided to conclude special Partnership and Cooperation agreements with the former Soviet republics (with the except of the three Baltic countries), and devised a separate aid programme, TACIS (Technical Assistance to the Commonwealth of Independent States). TACIS funds transborder cooperation in areas such as energy and transport (networks and infrastructure), environment and the fight against drug trafficking.

But encouraging regional cooperation among the former Soviet republics — particularly within the context of the Commonwealth of Independent States (CIS) — has been difficult for the EU: it has never considered signing an agreement with the CIS for the same reasons it would not do so with the CMEA during the 1970s and 1980s.[18] Doing so would legitimise and strengthen Russian control over its 'near abroad', a particularly sensitive issue for Georgia, Moldova and Ukraine above all. Furthermore, the prospects of regional cooperation have been slight because violent conflicts within and between them have been common (such as Armenia and Azerbaijan). As the Commission noted, these newly independent states "cannot be treated as a monolithic bloc", although they face common challenges (European Commission 2001b, 5).

The western former Soviet republics have been included in the 'European neighbourhood policy' (ENP), which is a clear attempt to delay further enlargement, and limit the implications of differentiation among new member states, those countries in the membership queue, and those clamouring to join the queue. In December 2002, the Copenhagen European Council launched the policy, aimed at Belarus, Moldova, Russia and Ukraine, and the southern Mediterranean countries; in June 2004, the Council extended the policy to the three Caucasian republics, Armenia, Azerbaijan and Georgia. Russia — the bull in the china shop — has since declined participation, preferring to develop cooperation with the EU on a more 'equal' basis.

According to the Commission, the ENP countries "should be offered the prospect of a stake in the EU's Internal Market and further integration and liberalisation to promote the free movement of persons, goods, services and capital" (European Commission 2003, 4). The EU will offer 'all but institutions' to the countries concerned, that is, all but EU membership (at least for the foreseeable future). Increased economic integration and closer political cooperation would be conditional, and clear benchmarks for each country would be set out. In 2004, the Commission began preparing individual action plans — detailing those benchmarks — for the most advanced neighbours. In December 2004, it published action plans for seven countries: Israel, Jordan, Moldova, Morocco, Palestinian Authority, Tunisia and Ukraine.[19] The action plans contain very long lists of 'priorities for action' (almost three hundred in the case of Ukraine), but in exchange do not actually offer clear incentives to the neighbours. The policy instruments available to the EU may in fact be inadequate to convince the neighbours to carry out the reforms the EU wants: for example, the Commission did not offer visa–free access to the EU, and most importantly, there is no 'magic carrot' of eventual EU membership, an issue which still dominates the relationship with some of the neighbours (especially Ukraine) since they have clearly and repeatedly expressed their wish to join the EU.

It is particularly notable that the European neighbourhood policy has hardly any strong regional component at all: the emphasis is not on encouraging the countries to cooperate with each other, but on encouraging each to undertake economic and political reforms. Bilateralism is clearly predominant over regionalism. There are, of course, the typical (for the EU) acknowledgements of the benefits of regional cooperation in the European Commission's communications on the ENP, but there is no overarching framework providing for regular meetings or contacts among all of the neighbours — even for those in the separate parts of Eastern Europe and the Mediterranean. The Mediterranean countries are, of course, all involved in the Euro–Mediterranean process, and the ENP does not replace it. But there is also remarkably little on regional cooperation in the action plans, compared to the emphasis on domestic reforms and building links with the EU. The action plans do encourage cross–border cooperation (neighbour to neighbour, and neighbour to EU member state), they do encourage political dialogue (between the EU and each neighbour) on 'regional issues', and they do encourage neighbours to free up their trade with each other. But such priority actions are vastly outnumbered by the actions related to domestic reforms.

Strikingly, the Commission has stated that the EU will "strongly encourage" regional integration in the Mediterranean, but will only "consider" new initiatives to encourage regional cooperation among the former Soviet republics (European Commission 2003, 8). It also made it clear that the EU will not establish new regional bodies but will, rather, support existing entities and thus support local ownership of regionalism (European Commission 2004, 21). Russia's self–exclusion from the ENP complicates matters; there is justifiable wariness about enhancing Russia's role in its 'near abroad', but without constructive Russian participation, sub–regional cooperation is stymied from the start. The lack of EU support for sub–regionalism does, however, go hand–in–hand with the preference of many of the EU's eastern neighbours to cut their own path to (eventual) EU membership. The trend is clearly towards more bilateralism rather than interregionalism in the EU's relations with its neighbours.

6. Conclusion

Interregionalism in the case of the EU's relations with Central and Eastern Europe floundered in the face of exigencies that favoured bilateralism. It was never a significant part of the EU's policy, both because the EU based that policy on conditionality (which requires bilateralism) and because the CEECs did not consider themselves to be a separate 'region'. Their aim was to join the EU, not to create sub–regional organisations that could serve as an alternative to EU membership, and that aim was, by and large, supported by the EU from an early stage. Bilateralism, in turn, had further profound implications for the enlargement process — implications which reverberate today in the EU's relations with other European countries.

Enlargement overshadows all attempts to encourage regional cooperation elsewhere in Europe: in southeastern Europe, this is clearly already the case. In the former Soviet Union, the EU has not actively encouraged sub–regionalism for fear of giving Russia too much of a dominant role in its 'near abroad' (a fear shared by most of the neighbours) and the ENP does not have a strong regional cooperation component. Given the inclusion of the southern Mediterranean countries in such a strongly bilateral ENP, the EU even risks signalling that it has reduced the importance of regional cooperation in the Mediterranean.

Paradoxically, the absence of interregionalism in Europe is resulting in an ever–larger EU, which makes it even more of a potentially powerful partner for other regional groupings around the world, provided an enlarged EU proves capable of functioning effectively. The success of regionalism in Europe largely depends on the capacity of the enlarged EU to reform itself, and therefore on the will of the EU member states to work together. If this does not turn out to be the case, we may rue the lost opportunity to have reshaped the 'architecture' of Europe as one of interlocking but strong interregionalisms.

Notes

1. 'Who speaks for the EU' varies according to policy area (trade, foreign policy, and so on), and the process of agreeing common policies can be quite hard going, leading sometimes to 'lowest common denominator' agreements. But this should not blind us to the fact that, on occasion, the EU can and does act as one in international relations.
2. 'European Community' is used here prior to the date of the Maastricht Treaty (1992) which transformed the European Community into the European Union.
3. PHARE stands for Poland/Hungary: Assistance for Restructuring Economies.
4. The break–up of Czechoslovakia on 1 January 1993 complicated matters, and the EU exercised pressure on both entities to ensure that it was peaceful. In October 1993 the EU concluded separate negotiations on Europe agreements with the Czech Republic and Slovakia.
5. Baldwin (1994), pp. 129–136. Between 1989 and 1994, for example, the share of Hungary's exports going to the EU increased from 33.8 to 63.7 per cent, while its share of exports to four Central and East European countries (Czechoslovakia, Poland, Bulgaria and Romania) decreased from 10.4 to 7.4 per cent. United Nations ECE (1996), p. 77.
6. *Agence Europe*, no. 5396, 20 December 1990.
7. The Visegrad group was formed primarily because the three countries wanted to join efforts to push for their accession to the European Community; see Torreblanca (2001), p. 143. At times, though, achieving cooperation within the group proved to be quite a challenge; see Fawn (2001).
8. European Council (1999), paragraph 4. This condition was aimed at Turkey in the first instance, but builds on previous declarations *vis–à–vis* the other applicants.
9. Figures from the CEI website, http://www.ceinet.org (accessed 1 February 2005).
10. Estonia seemed only a marginally (if at all) more suitable candidate than Latvia and Lithuania (as the latter two countries bitterly pointed out afterwards). The inclusion of only one Baltic country would expand the first round of enlargement but not in a threatening way, and would help reassure the Baltic republics that they were firmly within the EU's 'sphere of influence'.
11. European Commission (1999), p. 30. The Commission justified its recommendation by arguing that the six applicant countries met the *political* condition for membership (the most important), if not the other conditions. This provided a convenient way to handle Turkey's membership application:

negotiations would not open with Turkey because it did not (yet) meet the political condition, but Turkey would conclude an Accession Partnership with the EU.

12. European Council (2002), p. 4. This is striking, because previous European Councils had been so hesitant to set a definite date for the accession of specific candidates. The risks of alienating Bulgaria and Romania were considered too great *not* to give a firmer indication of when those two countries might finally accede.
13. Remarks by Tamás Szûcs, Hungarian Mission to the European Union (and a negotiator at the Copenhagen European Council which concluded the accession negotiations) to the University Association of Contemporary European Studies (UACES) conference on enlargement, 4 April 2003, King's College London.
14. The history of the Visegrad group is one of contrasting periods of activity and discord (see Fawn 2001), and the behaviour of the Visegrad countries in the membership negotiations seems to indicate a more recent period of discord.
15. CEFTA's website, however, mentions no major meetings since 2000 (http://www.cefta.org, accessed 1 February 2005) indicating that it was effectively defunct well before the 2004 EU enlargement.
16. The history of the Nordic Group (Norway, Iceland, Sweden, Finland, Denmark) after the 1995 EU enlargement to Sweden and Finland is instructive: once an active group at the UN, for example, it is now much less prominent than the EU (see Laatikainen 2003).
17. Article 6, Amsterdam Treaty available on the EU's website http://europa.eu.int (accessed 1 February 2005).
18. For a more positive view of the chances for interregionalism here, see Dupont and Engelen (2004), 174.
19. They are available on the European Commission's ENP website: http://europa.eu.int/comm/world/enp/document_en.htm (accessed 28 January 2005).

References

Adamiec, J. (1993) East–Central Europe and the European Community: A Polish Perspective, *RIIA Discussion Paper no. 47* (London: Royal Institute of International Affairs).

Andriessen, F. (1992) Europe and the World After 1992, Speech at the UK Presidency Conference, London, 7 September.

Bailes, A. J. K. (1999) The Role of Subregional Cooperation in Post–Cold War Europe: Integration, Security, Democracy, in: A. Cottey (ed.) *Subregional Cooperation in the New Europe: Building Security, Prosperity and Solidarity from the Barents to the Black Sea* (London: Macmillan).

Baldwin, R. (1994) *Towards an Integrated Europe* (London: Centre for Economic Policy Research).

Cottey, A. (1999) Conclusion, in: A. Cottey (ed.) *Subregional Cooperation in the New Europe: Building Security, Prosperity and Solidarity from the Barents to the Black Sea* (London: Macmillan).

Council of the European Union (1997) Conclusions on the principle of conditionality governing the development of the European Union's relations with certain countries of south–east Europe, 29 April, *EU Bulletin*, no. 4.

Council of the European Union (1999) Common Position of 17 May 1999 concerning the launching of the Stability Pact of the EU on south–eastern Europe, document no. 99/097, *European Foreign Policy Bulletin online*, available at: http://www.iue.it/EFPB/Welcome.html (accessed 1 February 2005)

Dunay, P. (2004) Strategy with fast-moving targets: East–Central Europe, in: R. Dannreuther (ed.) *European Union Foreign and Security Policy: Towards a Neighbourhood Strategy* (London: Routledge).

Dupont, C. & Engelen, H. D. (2004) Elusive Interregionalism: The European Union and Eastern Europe, in: V. K. Aggarwal & E. A. Fogarty (eds) *EU Trade Strategies: Between Regionalism and Globalism* (Houndmills: Palgrave Macmillan).

European Commission (2004) European Neighbourhood Policy Strategy Paper, COM (2004) 373 final, 12 May.

European Commission (2003) Wider Europe — Neighbourhood: A New Framework for Relations with our Eastern and Southern Neighbours, COM (2003) 104 final, 11 March.

European Commission (2001a) Making a Success of Enlargement: Strategy Paper 2001 and Report of the European Commission on the Progress Towards Accession by Each of the Candidate Countries, Brussels, 13 November.

European Commission (2001b) TACIS Regional Cooperation: Strategic Considerations 2002–2006 and Indicative Programme 2002–2003, 27 December.

European Commission (1999) Composite Paper: Reports on Progress Towards Accession by Each of the Candidate Countries, Brussels, 13 October.

European Commission (1997a) Agenda 2000: For a Stronger and Wider Union, *EU Bulletin Supplement 5/97*.

European Commission (1997b) Report on Regional Cooperation in Europe, COM (97) 659 final, 1 December.

European Commission (1996a) Report on the Current State of and Perspectives for Cooperation in the Baltic Sea Region, COM (96) 609 final/3, 21 February.

European Commission (1996b) Report on European Union Cooperation with the Central European Initiative (CEI), COM (96) 601 final, 4 December.

European Commission (1995a) Report to the General Affairs Council on the promotion of intra–regional cooperation and "bon voisinage", 6 March.

European Commission (1995b) Communication on European Community Support for Regional Economic Integration Efforts among Developing Countries, COM (95) 219 final, 16 June

European Council (2002) Copenhagen, Presidency Conclusions, 12–13 December, document no. SN 400/02.

European Council (1999) Helsinki, Presidency Conclusions, 10–11 December, *European Foreign Policy Bulletin online*, available at: http://www.iue.it/EFPB/Welcome.html (accessed 1 February 2005).

European Council (1996) Presidency Conclusions, Florence, 21–22 June, *European Foreign Policy Bulletin online*, available at: http://www.iue.it/EFPB/Welcome.html (accessed 1 February 2005).

European Council (1993) Conclusions of the Presidency, Copenhagen, 23–22 June, document no. SN 180/93.

Fawcett, L. (1995) Regionalism in Historical Perspective, in: L. Fawcett & A. Hurrell (eds.) *Regionalism in World Politics* (Oxford: Oxford University Press).

Fawn, R. (2001) The Elusive Defined? Visgrad Co-operation as the Contemporary Contours of Central Europe, *Geopolitics* 6(1).

Final Conference on the Pact on Stability in Europe (1995) Political Declaration adopted at the Conclusion of the Final Conference on the Pact on Stability in Europe and List of Good–Neighbourliness and Cooperation Agreements and Arrangements (1995), *EU Bulletin*, no. 3.

Finnish Presidency and the European Commission (1999) Report to the European Council on EU Action in support of the Stability Pact and south–eastern Europe, Press Release no. 13814/99, 6 December.

Körmendy, I. (1992) The Hungarian View: An EC Associate's Perspective from Central Europe, in: R. Rummel (ed.) *Toward Political Union: Planning a Common Foreign and Security Policy in the European Community* (Boulder: Westview).

Laatikainen, K. V. (2003) Norden's Eclipse: The Impact of the European Union's Common Foreign and Security Policy on the Nordic Group at the United Nations, *Cooperation and Conflict* 38(4).

Monar, J. (1997) Political Dialogue with Third Countries and Regional Political Groupings: The Fifteen as an Attractive Interlocutor, in: E. Regelsberger, P. de Schoutheete de Terverant, & W. Wessels (eds.) *Foreign Policy of the European Union: From EPC to CFSP and Beyond* (Boulder: Lynne Rienner).

Sjöstedt, G. (1977) *The External Role of the European Community* (Westmead: Saxon House).

Torreblanca, J. I. (2001) *The Reuniting of Europe: Promises, Negotiations and Compromises* (Aldershot: Ashgate).

United Nations Economic Commission for Europe (1996) *Economic Bulletin for Europe*, vol. 48 (Geneva: UNECE).

Verheugen, G. (2001) Debate on EU Enlargement in the European Parliament, Strasbourg, 4 September 2001, Rapid Document, SPEECH/01/363.

Appendix: Membership of Sub–regional Groupings in Europe

Visegrad group: Czech Republic, Hungary, Poland, Slovakia

Central European Free Trade Agreement (through 2004): Bulgaria, Czech Republic, Hungary, Poland, Romania, Slovakia, Slovenia

Council of Baltic Sea States: Denmark, Estonia, European Commission, Finland, Germany, Iceland, Latvia, Lithuania, Norway, Poland, Russia, Sweden

Barents Euro–Arctic Council: Denmark, European Commission, Finland, Iceland, Norway, Russia, Sweden

Black Sea Economic Cooperation: Albania, Armenia, Azerbaijan, Bulgaria, Georgia, Greece, Moldova, Romania, Russia, Turkey, Ukraine

Central European Initiative: Albania, Austria, Belarus, Bosnia–Herzegovina, Bulgaria, Croatia, Czech Republic, Hungary, Italy, Former Yugoslav Republic of Macedonia (FYROM), Moldova, Poland, Romania, Serbia–Montenegro, Slovakia, Slovenia, Ukraine

The EU as a Global Actor and the Dynamics of Interregionalism: a Comparative Analysis

FREDRIK SÖDERBAUM*, PATRIK STÅLGREN** & LUK VAN LANGENHOVE†

1. Introduction

This collection has focused on the EU's role as a global actor and the importance of interregionalism in its external activities. This is a fairly new development. During much of the 1960s the then European Communities had only limited relations mainly with former European colonies, and were slowly beginning to assert a common position on international trade (Smith

2003, 229). By contrast, today's EU has a wide range of economic, political, social and, increasingly, also cultural relations with virtually every continent and country in the world. Some of these relations are region–to–region and can be understood as interregionalism. As a result, the EU's "presence" is felt more or less everywhere, albeit more in some sectors and regions than in others (Bretherton & Vogler 1999). Many questions exist on the nature and impact of the EU's role as a global actor and player.

This collection of studies has provided theoretical and empirical insights into the EU's 'actorness' on the world scene. It took as a point of departure the fact that, during the last decade, there has been an increasing emphasis on interregionalism as a guiding principle for the EU's foreign policies and external relations. The proponents of this approach even speak of a European model or doctrine of global policy based on interregionalism (Hettne 2005; Verhofstadt 2001). This policy is implemented through a large number of interregional arrangements with regions around the world, several of which have been analysed in detail in this collection.

This concluding study offers a comparative analysis of the role of interregionalism in the EU's performance as a global actor. It draws heavily on the five case studies presented in this collection but also transcends them in order to provide a comprehensive assessment. The key focus is to try to explain some of the principal characteristics of the EU as a global actor, and to account for the variation in the policy of interregionalism across regions and sectors.

The analysis is structured in three main sections. As a common point of departure, a comparative overview of the role of interregionalism in the EU's foreign policy is provided. Then, the main section presents three partly over-lapping and intersecting explanations of the EU's foreign policies that account for the variation in the policy of interregionalism across regions: (i) promoting a liberal internationalist agenda; (ii) promoting the EU's identity as a global actor around the world; and (iii) promoting the EU's power and competitiveness. Finally, theoretical conclusions are drawn and some ingre-dients for an emerging research agenda on the study of the EU's foreign policy and interregionalism are put forward.

2. A Snapshot of EU–driven Interregionalism

Interregionalism has become a strong component of the EU's relations with Latin America, Asia and Africa. But, for reasons discussed in detail below, interregionalism is neither the guiding principle of the EU's relations with North America nor of those with the Central and Eastern European countries.

As Sebastian Santander points out, interregionalism is particularly strong in the EU's external policies towards Latin America, where the EU has inter-regional partnerships with most relevant sub–regions, such as the Andean region, Central America and, above all, Mercosur. The EU–Mercosur part-nership is one of the most developed cases of interregionalism that exists anywhere in the world. The origins of the partnership are in trade relations, and this aspect continues to be particularly strong through an interregional free trade agreement with quotas only in agriculture and some other sensitive goods. Gradually, however, the focus of interregional cooperation has widened to include other sectors such as economic cooperation and development cooperation, as well as political dialogue and exploration of common 'values'.

Although the EU–Mercosur partnership is of recent origin, interregionalism as such is not. The EU's relations with the African, Caribbean and Pacific (ACP) group of countries are testimony to a long history of interregionalism (albeit in a more loose form since the ACP is not a region). Mary Farrell shows that the historical focus in the EU–ACP partnership has been on humanitarian issues and a special trading relationship, but this is now being redefined. As seen in the Cotonou Agreement, there is a stronger emphasis on, for example, reciprocal trade, political conditionalities, supporting regionally based economic cooperation and integration, human rights and democracy, and the 'war on terror'.

For our purposes it is of particular importance to note that the EU differentiates between ACP countries and is in the process of establishing partnership agreements with more geographically focused sub–regional organisations of Africa, such as the Southern African Development Community (SADC) and the Economic Community of West African States (ECOWAS). This can be seen as a strengthening of and even a new step towards formal interregionalism. Former EU–ACP relations represented a looser form of interregionalism with quite a weak partner organisation and dealt with few sectors. Aggarwal and Fogarty refer to this as hybrid interregionalism.

According to Julie Gilson, the Asia–Europe Meeting (ASEM) also represents a new type of interregionalism, which must be understood as a post–Cold War phenomenon. As in the case of relations with Africa, EU–Asia interregionalism is comprehensive and multisectoral, spanning trade and investments, politics, security and anti–terrorism, culture, technology and science, drug trafficking, environmental protection and so on. An impressive variety of issues is included within the ASEM framework, but the agenda tends to be *ad hoc* in nature and rather flexible, even unfocused.

It is, thus, interesting to note that EU–driven interregionalism tends to be multifaceted and comprehensive in nature. Nevertheless, different issues and themes receive different attention in different regions. Interregional policy is, therefore, not a fixed set of guidelines but subject to adaptation. At the same time, it is important to note that interregionalism is not geared towards all regions. In fact, interregionalism characterises neither the EU's relations with North America nor those with the former Central and Eastern European countries.

With regard to the North American case, Aggarwal and Fogarty state that "even as the EU pursued interregional strategies toward many other ill–defined and weakly institutionalised 'regions', it avoided an interregional approach toward its most important commercial partner. Simply put, there is no discernable EU–North America relationship" (Aggarwal & Fogarty in this collection). Instead the EU is engaged in a series of bilateral relationships with Canada, Mexico and the United States rather than a genuine region–to–region link.

Referring to Central and Eastern Europe, Karen Smith argues that "[i]nter-regionalism did not figure much at all in the enlargement process: although ten countries joined the EU at the same time, they did not form a cohesive grouping" (Smith in this collection). Smith claims that even though the EU had an open approach and to some extent encouraged the formation of regional bodies prior to enlargement, the Eastern European countries celebrated their newly–won national independence and thus shied away from regional clusters in favour of bilateral engagements with the EU. She also shows that the Eastern European countries associated regional formations in their part of the world with the era of Soviet rule. In essence, enlargement overshadows an interregional approach.

3. Explaining EU Interregionalism

It is undisputed that no single theory can provide satisfactory answers to a comprehensive phenomenon such as the EU's interregional policy. Although other perspectives may also be relevant, this collection has underlined the continued relevance of the dominant theories in the discipline of international relations, that is, variants of realism and liberalism and also constructivist perspectives. In what follows below these three partly overlapping and intersecting perspectives are emphasised in accounting for the role of interregionalism in the EU's foreign policy and external relations, i.e., (i) the promotion of liberal internationalism; (ii) building the EU's identity as a global actor; and (iii) the promotion of the EU's power and competitiveness.

The Promotion of Liberal Internationalism

Many of the official statements and proclamations released by the European Commission underline the liberal and idealist underpinnings of the EU. As an example, one can refer to the conclusions of the European Council of June 2004 which stated that "the Union must continue to strengthen its leadership role in the fight against global poverty" (European Council 2004). Also, in a document outlining the EU's external relations the European Commission proudly states that:

> The EU is particularly active in promoting the human aspects of international relations, such as solidarity, human rights and democracy. ... the Union works with other countries and international organisations to bring everyone the benefits of open markets, economic growth and stability in an increasingly interdependent world. ... A major challenge now is to spread peace and security beyond the European Union's borders. To meet this challenge, the EU is developing a common foreign and security policy so that it can act as a force for stability, cooperation and understanding in the wider world (European Commission 2004a, 1 & 3).

The EU's external relations objectives, with a strong emphasis on the 'human' benefits of economic interdependence, democracy, human rights and the principles of sustainable and participatory development, are often referred to as a "liberal internationalist" approach to international relations (Smith 2003). The EU often proclaims solidarity as a foundation of its external relations. An example is the joint statement in November 2000 by the Council and the Commission on the European Community's Development Policy:

> The European Union provides approximately half of all public aid to the developing countries and is their main trading partner in many cases. Its activity covers all the regions of the world. This effort reflects the essential solidarity which is an underlying feature of its international activity. The exercise of such solidarity must be seen as a major political challenge. In accordance with the principles upon which it is based, the Union needs to put this message across in every forum and ensure that it is disseminated, particularly in other industrialised countries (European Commission 2000, 1).

The same policy document asserts that "Community action is more neutral than action by the Member States, which have their own history and are bound by a specific legal system. Community solidarity and the Community's integrated approach to cooperation are undoubtedly major assets" (European Commission 2000, 4). It is no exaggeration to say that the EU sees itself as a model for the rest of the world, in particular "as the ultimate expression of conflict resolution by economic means" (Kühnhardt 2003, 47).

The EU often proclaims that multilateral trade liberalisation is important for fostering not only economic growth but also environmentally sustainable development and social equality all over the world. As stated in a recent document from the Commission: "Freer trade can mean more business opportunities, more efficient allocation of resources and more wealth" (European Commission 2001a). According to the official discourse, this is stated to be particularly important for the countries in the south. In fact, a crucial ingredient in the EU's development strategy is to integrate developing countries into the global economy and to promote their own efforts at regional integration (European Commission 2001a). These objectives have led the EU to support regional integration efforts around the world and to enhance interregional cooperation. With regard to the ACP countries, the official strategy is stated as follows:

> ... the Union is combining trade and aid in a new way in the next generation of "economic partnership agreements", currently being negotiated with the ACP countries and due to be in place by 2008. The idea is to help the ACP countries integrate with their regional neighbours as a step towards global integration, and to help them build institutional capacities and apply principles of good governance. At the same time, the EU will continue to open its markets to products from the ACP group, and other developing countries (European Commission 2004a, 10).

Behind this statement is the belief that the EU should try to consolidate regional integration arrangements among developing countries *because* regional integration is seen as "an important step towards their integration in the world economy" (European Commission 2004a, 10). Besides helping developing countries to integrate into the world economy and among themselves, it is also believed in EU circles that regional integration and cooperation can enhance peace, prevent conflict and promote cross–border problem–solving and the better use and management of natural resources. Such ideas are also shared by global institutions such as the International Labour Organisation (ILO) and United Nations Development Programme (UNDP) who have stressed that regional integration can be a tool for managing the 'dark sides' of globalisation.

This shows that, in EU's view, fostering region–building and interregionalism has become important not only for the promotion of trade and aid but also as a means for comprehensive social and economic development on a global scale. The support and promotion of regional integration and cooperation has received recognition as one of six focal areas through which the EU can contribute to development around the world and in a range of different sectors (the others being: the linking of trade and development, support for macro–economic policies and promotion of equitable access to social services, transport, food security and sustainable rural development, and institutional capacity–building) (European Commission 2000).

In sum, promoting and even contributing to building regional integration schemes around the world serves a double function for the EU: on the one hand, it allows the human aspect and development issues to be brought into international relations, while, on the other hand, it creates entities that can start having relations with the EU as regions (i.e., ultimately, as regional actors).

Building the EU's Identity as a Global Actor

This section emphasises the attempts by the EU to build its identity as a global actor (which often, but not always, implies promoting interregionalism).

In the case of the EU's Asia strategy, which began in 2001, the EU's underlying interests were outlined in a straightforward manner which does not automatically correspond to the normative agenda of liberal internationalism outlined above: "There is one clear core objective to guide the future development of EU–Asia relations into the coming decade: we must focus on strengthening the EU's political and economic presence across the region, and raising this to a level commensurate with the growing global weight of an enlarged EU" (European Commission 2001b, 15).

This citation illustrates that the EU's foreign policy is also motivated by the promotion of the EU as a global actor through strengthening its "presence". Presence is intimately related to both identity building and "actorness" (Bretherton & Vogler 1999; Hettne 2005). The objectives of establishing "presence" and "actorness" have only recently become more salient for actors in the EU. Interestingly, the recent official introduction to a document outlining the EU's external relations states that:

> The EU did not set out to become a world power. Born in the aftermath of World War II, its first concern was bringing together the nations and peoples of Europe. But as the Union expanded and took on more responsibilities, it had to define its relationships with the rest of the world (European Commission 2004a, 3).

During the last decade it seems to have become evident in the Commission and in leading policy circles that the EU's increasing economic weight and geographical size are linked to an imperative to become a global actor by playing a more important political and security role in the world. Thus, in order to play such a global role in the world, it is necessary that the EU increases its 'actorness' and attains the qualities of an actor that is capable of making more autonomous foreign policy decisions. One of many examples of this trend was demonstrated at the Cologne European Council meeting in June 1999, where it was decided that "the Union must have the capacity for autonomous action" and this is only possible if it is backed up "by credible military forces, the means to decide to use them, and a readiness to do so, in order to respond to international crises without prejudice to actions by NATO" (European Council 2005).

There is a rather striking self–confidence within the EU regarding the importance of its own integration experiences for other regions as well as the 'need' for it to be/become a global actor. In an historical overview of the European Commission's activities it is stated that the Commission delegations serve the purpose of "taking both the idea and reality of European Union to a world *hungry for its presence*" (our emphasis) (European Commission 2004b, 59). This collection has demonstrated that the EU's attempts to promote interregionalism can at least partly be explained by a self–image that leads it to 'give' the EU to a world "hungry for its presence". Spreading the EU experience therefore implies promoting region–building around the world. The main vehicle for this project of external relations is, as the authors have argued, the principle of interregional relations. In other words, the building of the EU's identity as a global actor is closely related to and reinforced by a process of region–building and interregionalism. Interregionalism not only justifies and promotes the EU's 'actorness' (both within EU itself and to the rest of the word), but also strengthens the legitimacy of other regions which, in turn, promotes further region–building and cross–cutting patterns of interregionalism. Thus, the EU's preference for region–building and interregionalism has implications not only for the foreign policy of the EU, but also for the organisation of the world polity where regional actors such as the EU gain legitimacy.

A crucial ingredient in understanding the EU's role in the promotion of regionalism is its self–image as the 'natural' point of reference for regional initiatives. The EU tries to promote its own regional experience as the norm for region–building throughout the globe. The EU is eagerly persuading other regions, especially in Africa but also elsewhere, to follow its own example, which it sees as "a model for integration between countries in other regions of the world" (European Commission 2004a, 3). The EU is (consciously and unconsciously) projecting its own particular regional integration model to the rest of the world.

Although in official rhetoric the EU does not claim to 'export' the European integration model, its self–image as "the most advanced regional integration project in the world" is evident in a closer analysis of its policies and partnerships (European Commission 1995). In the same policy document, for example, the European model of integration is proclaimed as the most important reference model for virtually all regional initiatives in the world (especially in the south):

> There are a number of lessons that can be drawn from the experience of regional integration in various parts of the world. Probably the most important lesson can be derived from the European experience, not only on account of its long history but also because, to a large extent, it can be considered as the only successful example of regional integration so far (European Commission 1995, 8).

It should not be overlooked that the European integration experience is rooted in its own historical context and, as such, not automatically transferable to other parts of the world. Likewise, the relevance and transferability of the EU model is certainly contested, both among policy makers and in the research community. Many have pointed to the irrelevance and the ineffectiveness of a transfer of the EU model, especially to the south (Breslin & Higgott 2000, 343). Given the *sui generis* character of the European example, it is not possible to come up with 'empirical' evidence that backs the claim that the EU's experience with regional integration has some sort of universal applicability. But it is clear that, in promoting the EU experience as globally applicable, the EU's own identity and legitimacy as a global actor increases.

According to the official rhetoric, the 'human aspects' of international relations and the liberal internationalist agenda are often put forward as the main motives of the EU's foreign policy behaviour. This is closely linked to the so–called 'civilian power' argument, which has recently gained much favour in the research community. According to this view, the EU can be seen as a 'civilian power', pursuing a foreign policy which first and foremost stems from the values promoted internally within the Union, such as social pluralism, the rule of law, democracy and the market economy.[1] These values are seen as 'universal' and deemed to be part of a civilian as opposed to a militaristic foreign policy. A constructivist (and critical) analysis suggests that a so–called 'civilian' foreign policy can be part of a strategy to manifest the EU's identity as a benevolent global actor. Seen from this perspective, the EU's promotion of interregionalism as a model for its foreign relations is primarily a vehicle to gain international acceptance for the EU's own regional integration process rather than the humanitarian needs of the world. Interregionalism is then determined "by the ongoing need to forge a common European identity among the people of its constituent nations and by a belief in the utility of regions as a unit for organising the global economy" (Aggarwal and Fogarty 2004, 14). The way to achieve this is by actually creating regional integration schemes and regions elsewhere that can act as counterparts.

In a Westphalian world of states, the EU will always remain a special and somewhat isolated case. But in a world order where regions have a firm place next to states, the EU would be less isolated. To the extent that other regional actors primarily deal with the EU rather than with individual member states, integration will be reinforced. The EU's bid for interregionalism is, in this view, driven by an intraregional need to manifest the EU's regional experience as a globally accepted polity. This is linked to the idea of global legitimacy — the idea of emulating or even rejecting EU–style regionalism represents an explicit recognition of the EU's regional actorness.

Gilson emphasises the link between interregionalism and region–building. Her argument, developed with regard to ASEM, is that "the East Asian regional self acts itself into being" (Gilson in this collection). According to this view, interregionalism creates a global public reality, which not only structures interregional relations but also has a constitutive role in the formation of regions. Interregionalism creates and legitimises regional actors including, perhaps most significantly, the EU.

This section has suggested that one of the EU's main foreign policy objectives is to establish itself as a global actor and promote a world order where regions gain increasing legitimacy as actors in international affairs. Even though there is evidence to support the increasing use of interregionalism in the EU's foreign relations, relations with North America and former Eastern Europe provide contrasting cases. The authors argue, however, that these cases should not be understood as 'failures' of interregionalism. They show that interregionalism is not a programmatic doctrine for the EU, but rather a pragmatic strategy. These cases suggest that if there is a coherent 'doctrine' of the EU's foreign policy, the core objective is to establish the EU as a global actor. In the EU's relations with North America and Central and Eastern Europe interregionalism was not the appropriate means to this goal. In Central and Eastern Europe enlargement was the goal, but a bilateral approach overshadowed an interregional strategy. Nevertheless, in this context it is important to note that the enlargement process can be understood as a process of building and increasing the weight and size of the EU, which in turn enhances its identity as a global actor. In our view, this is not necessarily a failure of interregionalism, because enlargement and interregional relations are similar in that they both aim to increase the EU's actorness, and in fact are means towards that end. Thus, it is not only through its pro–regional and interregional policy that the EU is growing as a global actor, but also through the EU's 'bilateral' policies, for instance towards Russia, Ukraine, the United States, Canada and other big powers such as China.[2] As will be further discussed in the next section, there are strategic reasons for *not* pursuing interregionalism everywhere.

Strengthening the EU's Power

The goal to strengthen the EU's political power and to "defend its legitimate economic and commercial interests in the international arena" has started to appear more frequently in the justification of its foreign policy and external relations (European Commission 2004a, 3). The EU's common foreign and security policy (CFSP), which was introduced in 1993 by the Maastricht

Treaty following more than two decades of talk and looser cooperation, is at least partly geared towards strengthening the EU's political power so that it is more in tune with its economic power. The turn to power is also reflected in the so–called Lisbon agenda, which signals the EU's increased emphasis on strengthening its economic power position. According to this policy, the EU should strive to become the world's most competitive knowledge–based society while at the same time maintaining its social welfare system. It is difficult to dispute that the ambitions to strengthen political, military and economic power are not fully compatible with the high ideals and the normative agenda so often underlined in the official language concerned with the EU's external relations as an expression of "the human aspect of international relations" (European Commission 2004, 1).

In the analysis of the EU's search for increased power and competitiveness, attention is devoted to the strengthening of the EU's relative economic power, especially towards the USA and Japan, and the promotion of the EU's absolute economic power, which is often directed against the south.

Relative power: Many of the case studies in this collection have emphasised the fact that it is an important objective for the EU to strengthen its relative power position towards other global (regional and national) powers. Interregionalism — or the absence of it — has become a strategy to promote this goal. This is particularly evident in the EU's competition with the USA and Japan.

Santander argues, in his study of EU–Mercosur cooperation, that interregionalism is motivated by the EU's aim to play a global role and represent itself as a political union to its external partners. What is perhaps even more important in this context is the fact that Santander particularly emphasises the fact that the EU–Mercosur link is driven by the EU's aim to compete with and be a counterweight to the US in Latin America and globally. There is, therefore, a competition between EU–Mercosur cooperation and the US–driven project to create a Free Trade Area of the Americas (FTAA). Seen from this perspective, the EU's 'generous' interregional relations with Mercosur is a concession to Mercosur not only motivated by the EU's interests in Mercosur, but also the EU's competition with the USA, thereby giving rise to "competing regionalisms" (Hettne 2005). The same competitive dynamics are highlighted by Gilson, arguing that ASEM is used by the EU in order to strengthen EU–Asia relations and their "collective interest in restraining the US presence in Asia" (Gilson in this collection). From the EU's point of view, the ASEM is also garnering economic interests in East Asia (specifically by co–opting the business community into the formal structures of ASEM) and in promoting the global profile of the EU.

It is particularly interesting to note that power politics at the same time explains the lack of interregionalism in the EU–NAFTA relationship. Aggarwal and Fogarty underline that the lack of interregionalism is a result of the fact that the EU is, above all, concerned with its relative position to the US, and that there is no economic or functional need for enhanced interregionalism:

As the two main centres of established economic power in the world, each has a strategic incentive to secure export markets for its producers. The United States, whether in its creation of NAFTA, APEC, or an FTAA, presents a challenge to Europe's commercial position in the world. In this context, access to potentially lucrative markets is relative and, as its rationale for pursuing an FTA with Mexico (among others) suggests, the EU is very much concerned with its position relative to the United States (Aggarwal & Fogarty in this collection).

In addition, it can be argued that strengthened EU–NAFTA cooperation would strengthen the role of NAFTA as a regional player and, in the process, also increase the relative power position of the US as a result of American domination of NAFTA.

Absolute power. In the EU's interregional policies towards Africa and Mercosur there is a strong emphasis that interregionalism must conform to World Trade Organisation (WTO) rules and the WTO agenda (as seen in the two studies by Farrell and Santander in this collection). A closer integration of the African countries and regions into the global economy is seen, in the EU's official rhetoric, as the way for future trading relations as well as a development strategy which is of mutual gain both for the EU and for the weaker partner regions. "As the world's biggest trading partner, the EU is also determined to secure its international competitiveness while at the same time promoting global commerce through further liberalisation of "world trade rules" — a process that it believes will be of particular benefit to developing countries (European Commission 2004a, 3).

Nevertheless, the EU's stated intention to connect the ACP to the global arena of liberal economic and democratic interactions in order to promote development may also be seen as a means of hegemonic control. Farrell suggests that this is by no means the idealist agenda emphasised in official discourse, but a way to promote the EU's self-interest. She claims that the EU's agenda is not based on a concern for African development and the spread of cosmopolitan values but rather reveals the realist tendencies or self–interest of the EU. It represents "a triumph of realism over idealism". Farrell is particularly critical of the shift of emphasis in the partnership from aid to trade, and towards increased political conditionalities and the interregional political dialogue, which are means to establish hegemonic control. The new type of interregionalism is said to reinforce the power asymmetries between the ACP group of countries and the EU.

Santander reveals a quite similar picture in the EU–Mercosur partnership. The value–loaded motives of win–win cooperation through free interregional trade is emphasised hand in hand with greater economic self–interest to bolster the EU's presence and access to fast growing economies. The EU has a high degree of rhetorical commitment to free trade but keeps its high non–tariff barriers with regard to agricultural products, where the weaker partners have the most to gain. In other words, EU–Mercosur cooperation is an interregional relationship primarily built on the interests of the stronger.

In both Africa and South America, we are at the same time witnessing a redirection as the interregional partnership spreads to cover more political issues and norms.

> Issues such as human rights, democracy and the rule of law together with good governance had crept into earlier agreements, and were reinserted with greater vigour into the new agreement. This time, however, violations of these principles could lead to the suspension of cooperation (or of aid) under a non–execution clause that was inserted by the EU and against the wishes of the ACP states (Farrell in this collection).

In Africa, the EU makes use of a series of different instruments and means: institution–building and formal agreements (such as the Cotonou Agreement and various types of Partnership and Cooperation Agreements), but also conditionalities, incentives and aid. Through building institutions and establishing agreements, Farrell argues, "the European Union has established the channels through which it can convey its values, priorities and even special interests" (in this collection). In this sense, interregionalism is more of a means than an end in itself. Built on agreements and some institution–building, interregionalism legitimises and enhances liberalisation, deregulation, privatisation and access (i.e., economic goals). As Gilson points out, here it is also important to acknowledge the western norms embedded in ASEM's institutional structure. In fact, there is evidence that the EU is establishing interregional institutions in order to convey its own norms and interests.

In this context it is interesting to note the various ways whereby the EU promotes the interregional model in different regions. The differences in the EU approach towards Africa as compared to Asia are most striking; ASEM is frequently stated to be interregionalism among 'equals', which contrasts with the EU–ACP relationship, which is asserted as "a model for how rich countries can help poorer ones" (European Commission 2004a, 9). There are several other differences as well, reflected in a much stronger emphasis on market liberalisation and political conditionalities in relations with Africa as compared to Asia.

The EU–Asia partnership is seen more as a meeting place where much can "be gained from dialogue and exchange of best practice" (European Commission 2001b). In the EU's Asia strategy referred to above, it is stated that "there is no single 'European model' of social governance", a statement that is to be understood in the context of the EU placing little emphasis on good governance and human rights in its relations towards Asia, and the different views regarding opening of free markets and free trade (European Commission 2001b, 17). This is in sharp contrast with the EU–ACP (and to some extent EU–Latin America) relationships, where the EU places more emphasis on both economic and market–based liberalisation as well as the use of political conditionalities. Perhaps, rather obviously, this is also linked to questions of relevance, power and absolute gain. The EU cannot deny the contemporary relevance (and power) of key East Asian states. This is not the case of African states.

What this suggests is that whereas much of EU's interregional relations are conducted under the pretext of mutual benefits and win–win solutions, the distribution of these benefits seems to be a function of the relative power positions of the EU *vis–à–vis* its counterparts. The stronger the counterpart, the more concessions are given by the EU. With weaker 'partners', the EU dictates much more of the conditions for interregional cooperation. This seems to explain the difference between the EU's relations towards the relatively strong East Asian region, as opposed to the weak African regions, or even to South Asia, i.e., the EU also differentiates within regions to advance multi–tiered interregionalism. The relatively stronger East Asian region benefits from access to European markets and is, to a large extent, invited to an 'equal' partnership. With regard to East Asia there are few conditionalities attached to cooperation. Towards Africa, on the other hand, there are both economic and political conditionalities attached, and access is on the EU's own conditions. Mercosur seems to lie between the two extremes.

4. Conclusion

Since the mid and late 1980s we have witnessed an explosion of various forms of regionalisms and regionalist projects all over the world. The widening and deepening of the EU is perhaps the most debated example of this trend, but the increasing importance of regionalism around the world can hardly be neglected. This can be understood as a 'regionalist movement', which show a great variety in terms of diversity, comprehensiveness and impact on peace and development (Hettne 2005). It has become evident that the regionalist movement is consolidated as regions and regionalist projects become more active on the world scene.

This is not a surprising development. As regions consolidate and become stronger they are also likely to turn outward. Hence, it is to be expected that they will find it attractive to relate to other regions, because this will be both 'effective' and at the same time increase the legitimacy of their actorness as regions. At least to a certain extent, regions need to respond to the sheer momentum of interregionalism which, in turn, is advanced by the regionalist movement itself. The importance of the EU in this process cannot be overstated. In many ways contemporary interregionalism is triggered and promoted by the EU. For many regions the EU is perceived as model and it provides a map or a 'how to' guide for regional integration and (now) interregionalism. This is, in turn, applauded by the EU itself, especially the European Commission representatives, since it enhances the EU's actorness and legitimacy.

Although interregionalism is no novelty, it still needs to find its place in the research field. Based on the experience of this collection some ingredients of an emerging research agenda on interregionalism and the EU's role as a global actor can be outlined. Interregionalism is currently underrepresented in the research community. There is, therefore, a need for more research, and above all for various types of comparisons in combination with detailed case studies that map the different manifestations of interregionalism around the

world, even conceivably a systematised effort to monitor interregional relations worldwide. In fact, such endeavours are already emerging. For
instance, there is an increasing amount of research on EU–Asia interregionalism, partly sponsored or related to the ASEM process. EU–Latin America
relations are now monitored by the 'EU–Latin America Relations Observa-
tory' (OBREAL), a network of Latin American and European research insti-
tutes. Also the new EU–funded Network of Excellence on 'Global
Governance, Regionalisation and Regulation: the Role of the EU'
(GARNET) will engage in monitoring activities. It is difficult to exaggerate
the importance of such data–gathering and quantitative and qualitative analyses for advancing critical and policy–relevant knowledge in this field.

As noted above, this collection has emphasised that the European
Commission as a supranational agency plays an important role in the initia-
tion, enhancement and spread of interregionalism around the world. The
European Commission has the discretion as well as the capacity to develop
interregional policies in a number of fields without being overly dependent
on the European Council and the individual member states. Sometimes the
Council actively promotes interregionalism, and is backing up the Commission in this process. However, there are also examples where the Commission's preference for interregionalism is counteracted by the European
Council, as shown by Aggarwal and Fogarty, when explaining the failure of
EU–NAFTA interregionalism.

This suggests that more detailed research is needed on why and how the
EU promotes interregionalism (and the reasons why it does not). This collection has to a large extent underlined the continued relevance of liberalism,
constructivism and realism as useful tools for understanding the formation
of EU interregional policy. It seems that individually and collectively these
theoretical perspectives appear to demonstrate the strength or absence of an
EU interregional strategy in the selected cases. In future research there is a
need to more systemtically assess the relevance of each and every one of them
(and other perspectives). Furthermore, as suggested elsewhere by Aggarwal
and Fogarty (2004) the different perspectives can also be combined and
mixed with one another, opening up room for creative theorising.

A neglected issue in the research field, which has served as an inspiration
to this collection, is that interregionalism needs to be analysed in its own
right and not only within the framework of regionalism. In this sense interregionalism constitutes an additional level of interaction in the world system.
It provides new opportunities to deal with security issues and offers new
avenues for region–to–region interaction. Distinguishing between regionalism and interregionalism allows for research on how regionalism and interregionalism relate and impact on one another. A rather uncontroversial
proposition is that regionalism will give rise to interregionalism. This is
outlined in the Introduction to this collection through our distinction
between three generations of regionalism. However, several studies in this
volume draw attention to a more intriguing two–way relationship, revealing
that interregionalism can, at the same time, reinforce regionalism. Engaging
in interregionalism creates a need for regions to consolidate. According to

Gilson, the nascent regionalising endeavours in East Asia have been bolstered by the need for the now thirteen Asian countries to provide a collective response to interactions with the EU. By the same token, Santander shows that interregionalism between the EU and Mercosur is consolidating the Mercosur project itself.

The intriguing relationship between regionalism and interregionalism deserves to be further investigated. It is worth exploring whether regionalism in the twenty–first century will require functioning interregionalism. In what ways does interregionalism change the nature of regionalism? To what extent does interregionalism promote or hinder regionalist projects?

This collection has provided intriguing empirical evidence on the ways interregionalism impacts and even transforms multilateralism. It needs to be said that a multilateralism based on regions — a "regional multilateralism" according to Hettne — implies a different kind of multilateralism compared to the conventional Westphalian multilateralism based on nation–states as the principal actors (Hettne 2005). A regionally–based multilateralism implies relations between all relevant regional organisations, resulting in a distinct mode of global governance built on regions, which Hettne refers to as a "European world order" (Hettne 2005). This collection demonstrates that there are some trends pointing in this direction. But the picture is rather ambiguous since, at the same time, the EU is also a defender of multilateral principles built on the interaction between states rather than regions. In this sense the EU is promoting both 'regional multilateralism' (interregionalism) and conventional Westphalian multilateralism and bilateralism.

Here it is worth taking into account that, to an increasing extent, the EU is able to perform as an actor at a variety of levels in world affairs. For instance, the EU is reaching agreements with other states (bilateralism), acting within the UN framework and WTO (multilateralism) and at the same time engaging in constructing interregionalism. There is a pressing need for more research on the interactions between interregionalism and multilateralism and the related topic of the consequences of interregionalism for global governance and world order. This implies addressing questions such as: Can interregionalism be seen as part of new world order that moves away from both unipolarism and classical Westphalian multilateralism? Does it form part of a pattern of regions being part of the world order, and what are the impacts of conventional multilateralism? Apart from the relationship to multilateralism, the relationships between interregionalism and bilateralism are also intriguing. This collection has revealed that sometimes bilateralism and interregionalism compete, but that the two can also exist side by side or even be mutually reinforcing. In the EU's official rhetoric, bilateral policies are mainly targeted towards the largest and most important countries — such as the US, Russia, Japan, China, India and South Africa — which also play a particularly important role within each region. There is a pressing need for more research on the complex relationships between interregionalism and its relationships towards multilateralism, regionalism as well as bilateralism.

Notes

1. See, for example, Grimm (2002, 598ff). Also see Telò (2004) and Hettne (2004). As Grimm (2002, 598) points out, the EU as a civilian power is based on features such as rules and international law in foreign relations, international institution–building (with possible transfer of sovereignty), promotion of social justice and equality, conflict resolution through with military means as last resort; and multilateral cooperation.
2. Thanks to Karen Smith for emphasising this point.

References

Breslin, S. & R. Higgott (2000), Studying Regions: Learning from the Old, Constructing the New, *New Political Economy* 5(3), pp. 333–52.
Bretherton, C. and J. Vogler (1999) *Europe as a Global Actor* (London: Routledge).
European Commission (1995) European Community support for regional economic integration efforts among developing countries, communication from the Commission, 16 June.
European Commission (2000) Joint Statement by the Council and the Commission on the European Community's Development Policy, Brussels, November, available at: http://europa.eu.int/comm/development/body/theme/consultation (accessed 24 February 2005).
European Commission (2001a) The European Union and the World, Brussels, March, available at: http://www.delken.cec.eu.int/en/eu_global_player/4.htm (accessed 15 Febuary 2005).
European Commission (2001b) Europe and Asia: A Strategic Framework for Enhanced Partnerships, Communication from the Commission, COM(2001) 469, September 4.
European Commission (2004a) A World Player: The European Union's external relations, DG for Press and Communication, July.
European Commission (2004b) Taking Europe to the world — 50 years of the European Commission's External Service, DG External Relations, available at: http://europa.eu.int/comm/external_relations/library/publication.htm (accessed 15 February 2005).
European Council (2004) Brussels European Council 17 and 18 June 2004 Presidency Conclusions, DOC/04/2, 18 June, available at: http://europa.eu.int/rapid/pressReleasesAction.do?reference=DOC/04/2&format=HTML&aged=0&language=en&guiLanguage=en (accessed 15 February 2005).
European Council (2005) Policies: Security and Defence Policies, available at: http://ue.eu.int/cms3_fo/showPage.asp?id=261&lang=en&mode=g (accessed 21 January 2005).
Grimm, S. (2002) European Union's Policy–Making Towards Africa: Playing Twister Abroad, *Nord–Süd Aktuell* 4/2002 [Journal of the German Overseas Institute], pp. 589–604.
Hettne, B. (2004) Interregionalism and World Order, Paper presented at SGIR Fifth Pan–European International Relations Conference, The Hague, September 9–11.
Hettne, B. (2005) Reconstructing World Order, in M. Farrell, B. Hettne & L. van Langenhove (eds) *Global Politics of Regionalism* (London: Pluto Press).
Kühnhardt, L. (2003) Contrasting Transatlantic Interpretations. The EU and the US towards a Common Global Role (Stockholm: Swedish Institute for European Policy Studies), p. 47.
Smith, K. (2003) EU external relations, in M. Cini (ed.) *European Union Politics* (Oxford: Oxford University Press).
Telò, M. (2004) Interregionalism as a Distinctive Feature of the Civilian Power of EU's Foreign Policy, Paper presented at SGIR Fifth Pan–European International Relations Conference, The Hague, September 9–11.
Verhofstadt, G. (2001) The Paradox of Anti–Globalisation, *The Guardian*, September 28.

Index

absolute power 127–9
accession process 106, 107
ACP countries *see* African, Caribbean and Pacific (ACP) countries
actorness *see* actors
actors: and bilateralism 10–11; definition 100; EU's role 3, 17, 40; global 5, 8–9, 10–11; purpose of the studies 3–5; and regional groups 50; and states 10; transnational 10, *see also* global role
Africa: asymmetry in EU relations 19, 20, 127, 128, 129; conclusions 31–2; and conditionality clauses 20, 28; and the Cotonou Agreement 3, 15–16, 20–3, 24, 30, 31; and democracy requirements 28, 128; development 20; and EU partnership model 16–17, 19, 21, 23; EU self-interest 18, 19, 127, 128; and the global economy 22; and international relations theory 16; and liberalisation 31; and the Lomé agreements 10, 17, 19, 20; multi level governance 26–7; political regimes 28; poverty 18; and regional integration 25–7; sovereignty 25–6; sub-Saharan 30, *see also* African, Caribbean and Pacific (ACP) countries; African Union (AU)
African, Caribbean and Pacific (ACP) countries: conclusions 31–2, 128, 129; and the Cotonou Agreement 3, 17, 22–3, 27, 32; and democracy 22, 27, 28, 128; and development 20; and intellectual property rights 31; and interregionalism 119, 121; and local government 24; and the Lomé agreements 17, 19–20; regional groupings 21, 22; and trade 20, 21, *see also* Africa; African Union (AU)
African Union (AU) 25, 26, 27
Agenda 2000 (European Commission, 1997) 105, 106
Agreement on Textiles and Clothing (WTO) 88

agreements *see* international agreements
agricultural exports 48, 49, 52, 53, 118
agriculture 48, 49, 51
aid: and Africa 20, 29, 32; and Asia 71; and Central and Eastern European countries 102; and human rights 27; and interregionalism 121; and southeast European countries 109–10
America *see* United States of America
Andean Pact 42
Andriessen, F. 103
anti-terrorism *see* terrorism
APEC *see* Asia-Pacific Economic Cooperation
APT *see* Association of South East Asian Nations
Argentina 41, 44, 46, 47, 49, 50
Argentine convertibility plan (1991) 46
ASEM *see* Asia-Europe Meetings
Asia: and aid 71; bilateral relations with EU 64, 70, 73–4; currency crisis 66, 72; identity 60, 72–6, 131; and interregionalism 119, 128; overview 2–3, 59–61; research 130; role of EU 60, 62–4, 71, 126; social/cultural issues 68; strategic papers 69; trade relations 74; and the USA 89, 126; values 73, *see also* Asia-Europe Meetings; East Asia; South Asia; Southeast Asia; *and specific countries*
Asia-Europe Business Forum (AEBF) 67–8
Asia-Europe Meetings (ASEMs): conclusions 73–6, 126; development 65–6; economic and political significance 60, 61, 65; and enlargement 2–3; inception 2, 64–5; and interregionalism 119, 128; and multilateralism 60; and non-governmental organisations 67–9, 75; overview 66–7; significance for USA 89, 126, *see also* Asia; Association of South East Asian Nations (ASEAN)
Asia-Europe People's Forums (AEPF) 68–9

dependence on the EU 43–4, 45, 47–8;
economic policies 41, 46; EU self-
interest 47, 127; free trade areas 10, 48,
49, 118; and global governance 38, 126;
and group-to-group dialogue 42, 43–54;
identity 131; international credibility
54; interregional framework 2; legal
status 46; and liberalisation 50, 51; and
neo-liberalism 41; problem of USA
domination 44, 45, 50, 89; role of
private capital 46; social issues 46; and
trade 42, 43, 45, 46, 48, 118
Mercosur-European Business Forum
(MEBF) 47
Mexico 50, 80, 83–4
Miami compromise (2003) 52, 53
Ministerial Conference of Seattle (WTO,
1999) 51
model of integration 123–4
model of partnership 16–17, 19, 23, 60
MOFA (Japanese Ministry of Foreign
Affairs) 60
multi-level governance model 8
multilateralism: and Asia-Europe 60; and
the EU 17, 92; and interregionalism 4,
38, 121, 131; and trade liberalisation
46, 53; and trade preferences 21
Mutual Recognition Agreements (MRAs,
1997) 82
Myanmar 65, 66

NAFTA *see* North American Free Trade
Agreement
nation-state 5, 8
neo-interregionalism 42, 43
neo-liberalism 30, 32, 41, 43
New Partnership for Africa's Development
(NEPAD) 25
New Transatlantic Agenda (NTA, 1995)
81
non-governmental organisations (NGOs)
67–9, 75
non-tariff barriers 49, 85
North America: absence of
interregionalism 80, 126; commercial
relations with the EU 80–6; conclusions
92–5, 119; overview 79–80, *see also*
Canada; Mexico; United States of
America
North American Free Trade Agreement
(NAFTA): and dominance of the USA

85; non-tariff barriers 85; origins 80;
relations with Argentina 44; relations
with the EU 84–6; significance 85–6

open regionalism 8
origins: of interregionalism 5–9
other: definition 61–2, 70
Ouro Preto summit (1994) 45

Pact for Stability (EU, 1994–5) 105
partnership model 16–17, 19, 23, 60
Patten, C. 59
peace 16, 42
PHARE *see* Poland/Hungary: Assistance
for Restructuring Economies (PHARE)
Plan Real (Brazil, 1994) 46
Poland 106–7
Poland/Hungary: Assistance for
Restructuring Economies (PHARE) 103,
105
political dialogue: in Central America 42,
45, 51; and interregionalism 3;
transatlantic 81, 82, 87; and the Treaty
of Maastricht 41
politics: power 4, 89–90, 125–9; and role
of interregionalism 4; and self-interest
16, 127, 128, 129; and shaping of Asia
60; and the USA 89–90, 126
poverty reduction 3, 18, 28, 30
power: asymmetry 19, 20, 23, 24, 32; and
EU foreign policies 4; strengthening
125–6
private capital 46
private sector 10
public sector 30–1

realism 5, 16, 17–18
region-to-region relations 2, 38, 61–2, 89
regional cooperation 101–2, 103–4
regional governance model 44
regional identity 72–6, 101
regional integration 7, 18, 25–7, 122
regionalism: at a global level 2, 9, 50; in
Central and Eastern Europe 100, 101;
conclusions 129; definition 100; and
enlargement 110; European 39–40; and
globalisation 7, 8, 41–2, 54; ideology 3;
and interregionalism 6–9, 130–1; in
Latin America 38–41; and non-
economic matters 7; overview 6–9,
37–8; and security 7; significance for

Treaty of Rome (1958) 19
Treaty of Westphalia (1648) 5
tripolarisation 65

unilateralism 17, 92
United States of America (USA):
  agricultural issues 52; and Asia 89;
  bilateralism 51–2, 79, 88–9, 94;
  conclusions 92–5; dominance 85, 86, 94;
  economy 39, 81–2; and genetically
  modified foods 88; and international
  relations 17; investment 81; military
  might 17, 92; power politics 89–90, 126;
  relationship with Argentina 44, 45, 49,
  50; relationship with EU 51, 81–2, 90–2,
  126; and the South American bloc 51,
  52, 54; and terrorism 52, 81; and trade
  40, 49, 83–4, *see also* North America;
  North American Free Trade Agreement
  (NAFTA)

Verhofstadt, G. 2
violations 23–4
Visegrad group 103, 105
Vision Group 66

welfare systems 126
Westphalian system 5–6, 7–8
world actor *see* global role
world economy 40, 122
world market 6
world order: and the collapse of
  communism 7–8; foreign policies 4; and
  interregionalism 9, 131; and regionalism
  8
World Trade Organisation (WTO): and
  agricultural issues 52; failure at Cancun
  52, 53; and global trading orders 21;
  Ministerial Conference of Seattle (1999)
  51; and property rights 31; rules 127;
  trade negotiations 40–1

For Product Safety Concerns and Information please contact our EU
representative GPSR@taylorandfrancis.com
Taylor & Francis Verlag GmbH, Kaufingerstraße 24, 80331 München, Germany

www.ingramcontent.com/pod-product-compliance
Lightning Source LLC
Chambersburg PA
CBHW081436270326
41932CB00019B/3224